PCredibility
OWER

The Art of Selling Yourself

By Richard Hansen and Allyn Kramer
With Larry Upshaw

Published by
Prestonwood Press
Dallas, Texas

A softcover original published by

Prestonwood Press
P.O. Box 795892
Dallas, Texas 75379

To purchase individual copies or for volume discounts, visit our Web site at www.credibilitypower.com or write us at the address above.

Credibility Power
The Art of Selling Yourself

© 2001 by Allyn Kramer and Richard Hansen

All rights reserved. Written permission must be secured from the publisher to use or reproduce any part of this book in any form or by any means, electronic, mechanical, photocopying, recording or otherwise, including storage in a retrieval system, except for brief quotations in reviews or articles.

ISBN 0-9634221-2-X

Library of Congress Catalogue Card Number 00-135732

Manufactured in the United States of America

10 9 8 7 6 5 4 3 2 1

Table of Contents

Introduction
Acknowledgments
About the Authors

PART ONE
How to Gain the Motivation to Use Credibility Power

Chapter 1
Anyone Can Harness the Power of Credibility 16
    Credibility Profile: *Larry North, Fitness Guru*
    What Is Credibility Power?
    Who Can Effectively Use Credibility Power?
    What Factors Inspire Credibility Power?
    A Media Explosion
    The Demand for Information
    The Desktop Publishing Revolution
    Many Potential CP Practitioners

Chapter 2
Moving From Expertise to Authority 29
    Credibility Profile: *Martha Stewart, Domestic Expert*
    CP Begins With the Right Expertise
    Personality Is Important
    Credibility Power at the Cutting Edge
    Strong Statements, Well Researched

Chapter 3
What's the Payoff ? 38

Credibility Profile: *Ike Vanden Eykel, Authority on Divorce*
Earning Big Bucks from CP
    Carl Sewell: Books Can Sell Faster than Cars
Personal Status
    Michael Bohdan: The Bug Man Proves <u>Anyone</u>
Can Become a Trusted Authority
Helping Others
    Morris Dees: From Direct Mail to a Direct Call for Justice

Chapter 4
Credibility Role Models: Learning from the Best 50

Credibility Profile: *Dottie Walters, An Unlikely Saga*
Model 1 — The Evolutionary Expert: **Neil Sperry**
Model 2 — The Accidental Expert: ***Dr. Phil McGraw***
Model 3 — Professional on the Prowl: ***Tom Hopkins***
Model 4 — Celebrity Appeal: ***Bruce Jenner***
Model 5 — The Inevitable Expert:
    Colin Powell, Norman Schwarzkopf

Chapter 5
Five Keys to Developing Expertise into a Marketable Asset 74

Credibility Profile: *Bob Bauer, A Corporate Star Is Born*
Key #1: Overcoming Obstacles
    Leon Simon: Sports and the Gift of Gab
Key #2: The Importance of Desire
Key #3: Getting There First
Key #4: Researching the Product
Key #5: Focusing Your Effort
    Martin Birnbach: His Job Is Finding Your Job

PART TWO

How to Set Credibility Power into Motion

Chapter 6
Getting Started   88

Credibility Profile: *Benjamin Dover, Credit Commentator*
Begin With Organization
Select the Correct Media
Know Your Limitations
Set Goals
Plow Right In

Chapter 7
Creating the Winning Product: Yourself   104

Credibility Profile: *Zig Ziglar, Mr. Positive*
Create a Unique Persona
   Ahron Katz: His Company with the Little Red Trucks
   Carol Miller: Enhance the Trust Factor
Understand the Market
   Bill Bishop: Getting What You're Worth
Take Risks
   Clyde Goldberg: Rolling the Dice on a Media Career

Chapter 8
CP's Top Tool: The Written Word   120

Credibility Profile: *Ken Fisher, Forbes Columnist*
Traditional Book Publishing
The New Book Business
   Dr. Alan Perlis: Can One Book Be Like Another?
Self-Publishing
   Benjamin Kaplan: Given the Choice, He'll Publish Himself

Newsletter Concept
Newsletter Production
Media Relations

Chapter 9
Other Tools for Cashing In 150

Credibility Profile: *Dr. Mark Bernstien, CP in Medicine*
Public Speaking
Seminars and Workshops
   Ken Bradford: Leveraging Seminars into
   Other Credibility Ventures
Audiocassettes/Videotapes/Software
   Vince Poscente: Down a Steep Slope and
   Around a Learning Curve
Radio and Television
Paid Programming

Chapter 10
Seeking Outside Assistance 168

Credibility Profile: *John Wood, Author/Professional*
Editors and Ghostwriters
Literary and Talent Agents
Collaborative or Subsidy Publishers
Graphic Designers
Public Relations Consultants
Video, Film and Audio Production
Finding the Right Promotional Hook

Chapter 11
Boosting Exposure 194

Credibility Profile: *Dr. Laligam Sekhar, Media-Savvy Neurologist*
Making Fame
How to Secure Media Coverage
The Basic Press Release

Make A Book Signing Your Own Private Party
Newspaper Reviews are Scarce but Valuable
On Television, Coffee Talk Sells Books
Making Your Plea on Radio
The Time for Paid Ads
Leveraging One Medium into Another
Second Printings, New Editions and More

PART THREE
How to Turn On Credibility Power and Keep it On

Chapter 12
Harnessing the Credibility of A Third Party   218

Credibility Profile: *John Haslett, Consumer's Friend*
Why Organizations Endorse Outside Providers
How Organizations Grant Endorsements
    Scudder Hits Endorsement Mother Lode
Benefits of Receiving Third-Party Endorsements
Which Endorsements to Seek
Endorsements Enhance Professional Services Marketing
Book Endorsements
Enhanced Public Standing

Chapter 13
High-Tech Uses of Credibility Power   230

Credibility Profile: *Drs. Jeff Siegel and Mike Gottlieb, Psychologist/Entrepreneurs*
Other Uses of the Internet
Selling E-Books
    Hugh Gardner: From Streamside to the Satellite
Books on Demand

Chapter 14
Maintaining Success 240

Credibility Profiles:
Mark Victor Hansen, The Master Motivator
Jack Canfield, The Dean of Self-Esteem
Master Your Subject
Court the Media
Expand the Franchise
Stay Fresh and New
Create Synergy
Be Realistic
Live Up to Commitments
Don't Make Overreaching Claims

Chapter 15
You've Got the Power — Now Use It! 254

Appendices	259
Index	266
The Partnership for Credibility Power	272

Introduction

"Hey, this credibility stuff is really powerful."

That's what Allyn Kramer remembers thinking as he held a $2,000 check sent to him by a potential customer. Allyn had never met the man and didn't know what he was supposed to do for the money. That was the joy of it. It seemed like found money at the time.

Allyn had just written and published a book on direct marketing called *How to Master the Art of Lead Generation*. He wrote the book while waiting out a non-compete agreement after selling his business. The purpose of the book was to gain credibility. He figured that when he went back into business, he wouldn't have to start from scratch if he had something that would instantly re-establish his credentials. He was now the author of a book on a subject dear to the hearts of those who need direct marketing services. Would the book be enough to prove his credibility?

The check in his hand proved the worthiness of his strategy. The money came after he had sent potential clients a newsletter promoting his book and explaining how people could buy it.

A few weeks after the newsletter went out, the check for $2,000 arrived. There was no note, just the check made out to Kramer Lead Marketing Group. Fortunately, the sender had his name, address and telephone number printed at the top of the check. Otherwise, Allyn would have had no idea how to contact him.

When Allyn called, he said to the man: "Thank you for the check. What do you want me to do for you?"

"I don't know," the man replied. "You wrote the book. You're the expert. Do what you think is best for me."

CREDIBILITY POWER

This man sent the money because he considered Allyn an expert who had written a book on a subject the man considered very important to his business. The two men had never met. This customer hadn't spoken to any of past clients or contacted Dun and Bradstreet. The fact that Allyn wrote a book was all he needed to know.

At that moment, Allyn realized how creating our own media can allow us to harness knowledge, skills and experience and use the power of credibility. Those media can be books, newsletters, newspaper and magazine articles, radio and television broadcasts, audio and videotapes, speeches, seminars or workshops.

The phenomenon that Allyn had tapped into, the power of credibility, really boils down to trust. The mysterious new customer trusted that he knew exactly how it should be spent. This belief was based solely on the fact that Allyn was a published author of a book on direct marketing.

As you might imagine, Allyn was delighted with the thought that he could write a book and checks would rain down on him. Before he could justify publishing this book on marketing through the power of credibility, though, he needed to find out if others could duplicate his experience. To test out the phenomenon that has come to be known as Credibility Power (CP), he teamed with Dr. Richard Hansen, who recently retired as a professor of marketing at Southern Methodist University's Cox School of Business. Dick is now vice president of marketing and strategic planning for a large national financial services corporation.

Allyn and Dick spent countless hours discussing the power of credibility, the people who can use it and in what industries, and how Credibility Power can pay off for those who use it well. From these discussions came the suggestion that *anyone* with a passion for his work, who is willing to apply himself and be persistent, can benefit from the process of credibility marketing. A partnership was born to research and write this book.

This work is based on a straightforward premise: Anyone who has acquired some degree of expertise in a subject of interest to others can cash in. The range of expertise suitable for a venture into the power of credibility is as varied as the yellow pages. It extends from academics to insurance, from law to pest control to sales.

Credibility Power will describe how to accomplish your dreams — more money, enhanced status or a greater ability to help yourself and others.

* * *

There are many examples of people who have used the power of credibility to enhance their careers and lead full, rich lives. That's where the process of writing this book began, with interviews and research into the career paths of more than 40 people who have taken advantage of this power.

For purposes of this work, there are three distinct levels of success using Credibility Power. The top level includes such nationally-recognized figures as domestic expert Martha Stewart, former Olympic decathlon champion Bruce Jenner, motivational guru Zig Ziglar, *Chicken Soup for the Soul* author Mark Victor Hansen and business analyst Tom Peters.

The second level includes people who've reached wide acclaim among a more limited audience, such as motivational speaker and speakers' bureau promoter Dottie Walters, fitness expert Larry North, investment analyst and *Forbes* magazine columnist Ken Fisher, divorce attorney Ike Vanden Eykel, corporate scientist Bob Bauer and sales trainer Tom Hopkins. On the third level are people who have benefited on a state or local level. These include retirement specialist John Haslett, pest control expert Michael Bohdan, gardening authority Neil Sperry, sports talk show commentator Leon Simon, appliance fix-it man Ahron Katz and insurance salesman Clyde Goldberg.

The local experts could be from any large city. They serve as examples of how CP can be used on a local level in cities all across the country. These examples are meant to spur thought about the opportunities available in your own community. Is there a local gardening expert or an authority on consumer credit in your immediate area? Perhaps you could become that expert for your city. The authors present many such examples of Credibility Power at work and hope that everyone can learn from them.

Beginning with information from these sources, the authors have crafted a step-by-step guide that will allow anyone with a story to tell or a salable skill to make more money, earn enhanced status and achieve greater personal satisfaction. Now is absolutely the right time to employ the power of credibility. Read on and learn the uses of this valuable resource.

— Larry Upshaw

Acknowledgments

As people become successful, it's amazing how generous they become with their time, effort and ideas. We want to thank the many top professionals, all of whom are using the principles of Credibility Power, for granting interviews or otherwise participating in the research for this book. Their energy and enthusiasm was essential in our effort to inspire people to employ those principles and harness the power of credibility.

A special word of thanks goes to famed public speaker Dottie Walters, for allowing us to peek "behind the curtain" at the many details and procedures that make a book like ours successful.

To our editor, Lori Fairchild, we appreciate every red mark made on our manuscript and each suggestion to improve the content. The same goes to agent Randy Voorhees, who helped us with the book's title. We owe a special debt of gratitude to graphic designer Mike Fuld, who produced a package we feel is both reader friendly and emphasizes the challenging ideas in the book.

Larry Upshaw handled the difficult task of overseeing production of the book. With more than three decades as a magazine and newspaper writer, author and publisher, he understood from the outset how to bring our theory of Credibility Power to print. Upshaw is also president of his own professional services marketing firm, Professional Solutions Group, and his wide-ranging experience added credibility to our venture.

Thanks also to our many family members and friends, who kept us on track with editing suggestions and reviews of our work.

— The Authors

About the Authors

Dr. Richard W. Hansen received his Ph.D. from the University of Minnesota. He was a professor of marketing at the Cox School of Business at Southern Methodist University from 1972 to 1998 and also served on the faculties at three other universities — Wisconsin (Madison), Florida State and Arizona.

In addition to his academic career, Hansen is a well-known business consultant whose clients include Ford Motor Company, Honda, Texas Instruments, Prudential Realty Group, Fannie Mae, Yamaha, Chicago Title and Chicago Trust. He is also author or co-author of numerous research articles.

He is now vice president of marketing and strategic planning for United General Title Insurance Company.

* * *

Allyn Kramer is president of Kramer Lead Marketing Group, a multimillion-dollar direct marketing company headquartered in Dallas, Texas and recipient of the *INC* 500 award as one of the fastest-growing privately held companies in America.

Kramer's background includes direct marketing positions with Neiman-Marcus, The Drawing Board and TRW. He is the author of the best-selling book, *How to Master the Art of Lead Generation*.

He is a graduate of Drake University, holds an MBA and has taught college courses in direct marketing. He is a popular speaker nationwide on lead generation and direct marketing.

PART ONE

How to Gain the Motivation To Use Credibility Power

CHAPTER 1

IN THIS CHAPTER
- What is Credibility Power?
- Who Can Use Credibility Power?
- What Inspires Credibility Power?
- A Media Explosion
- The Demand for Information
- The Desktop Publishing Revolution
- More CP Practitioners

Anyone Can Harness the Power Of Credibility

Credibility Power is the dynamic, life-changing result of organizing and promoting a person's expertise into a position of recognized trust and authority. Its time has come and <u>anyone</u> can use it effectively.

ANYONE CAN HARNESS THE POWER OF CREDIBILITY

> **CREDIBILITY PROFILE**
>
> Fitness guru Larry North is one of the nation's foremost advocates of a fit and healthy lifestyle. A former personal trainer, North is an author, radio and television commentator, product pitchman and business executive. His story proves that with passion and persistence, it is possible for anyone to harness the power of credibility.

There is a yearning deep in the hearts of many businesspeople like Larry North. It is a passion, a desire that is even more important to success than talent, good looks or business savvy. North has all of these qualities, but his success is mostly a matter of "want to."

"Back in 1981, I was just another personal trainer," North recalls. "Only the very wealthy were using trainers then, but I saw there were a lot more people who needed help and weren't rich."

North had a definite goal. He wanted to become an acknowledged and trusted authority on the subject of fitness. He had the expertise. What he needed was the acknowledgment. So he sought help from one of his clients, a successful public relations agent. While North taught her the joys of exercise, she told him how to promote himself. In the process, North discovered how the principles behind Credibility Power can transform anyone from an average working person into a distinguished, respected authority in almost any line of work.

"I worked two days a week in my client's PR agency, and that's how I learned to self-promote," North says. "I decided to convince radio stations to use me as an expert on fitness. At first, I didn't feel confident promoting myself, so I would call the program directors and say I was someone else from the agency promoting Larry North."

Eventually, he talked his way into occasional spots on a top radio station. Then he became a regular on the station and leveraged his way onto an afternoon TV magazine show and a morning "coffee talk" program.

As his name became better known in the fitness industry, he attracted investors to his plan for a chain of fitness centers, sports medicine clinics, a restaurant and an equipment store. It seemed like the random action of word-of-mouth spread his name and abilities everywhere. Friends told him they saw and heard his name wherever they went. But this wasn't accidental. It was a calculated campaign generated by North himself.

"I would talk to restaurant owners and offer to develop a dish of nutritious, fat-restricted food that would go along with the other dishes on their menu," he explains. "That way I provided a valuable addition to their business — the Larry North Plate — and they helped me get my name before more people. And it didn't cost either of us anything."

North's outgoing personality earned him new opportunities, but it was his persistence that made him successful. When he first made an infomercial for exercise equipment, he hosted a program owned by a production company. But production values and a genial host are not the measures of a successful infomercial. The amount of sales generated is most important, and this series of programs was not making money.

North believed the programs had promise, if handled correctly. He and his investors purchased them, made a few changes and took charge of the promotion. The result has been a modern sales miracle. His infomercials are some of the largest moneymakers in the industry.

When North decided to do a fitness book, he put together a team that produced *Living Lean: The Larry North Program* and *Larry North's Slimdown for Life*. Both books feature North's photo on the cover as well as his name in the title. These projects followed a prime rule for establishing Credibility Power — keep your name and face before the public whenever possible.

"The books make some money," North notes, "but they are more for name identification." Successful marketing of the Larry North name has helped him attract investment to a chain of fitness clubs for a high-income group of 35- to 55-year-old exercise enthusiasts. And he has signed to market a line of energy bars in the nationwide chain of 7-Eleven convenience stores.

Today, there are thousands of personal trainers working in fitness centers throughout the country. With boundless energy and a positive outlook, Larry North has positioned himself as one of the foremost authorities among them.

What Is Credibility Power?

Credibility Power is the result of organizing and promoting your expertise, knowledge, skills and experience into a position of recognized trust and authority. It is accomplished through the use of today's media — writing and publishing books, giving seminars and workshops, contributing to radio and television programming, writing for newspapers and magazines, and publishing newsletters.

The use of CP may begin with a germ of an idea or a fully fleshed-out business strategy. The goal may be to increase revenue, respect or position in your current business or profession. Or you may want to use it to power a leap into a new career opportunity that demands enhanced knowledge or new skills. Credibility holds immense power to exploit a position of trust and authority.

The drive to market is as old as the desire to sell products and services. Every method of marketing has evolved from word-of-mouth. It all began hundreds of years ago when a tavern owner asked a satisfied customer to recommend his establishment to others, or a seamstress showed her wares to a wealthy person in hopes of earning additional rich patrons.

In the early days of our nation, word-of-mouth gave way to the first paid advertisements as newspapers and magazines came into being. People believed the claims made in these ads. We've all heard the outdated notion that if you read it in the newspaper, it must be true. The same held for paid

> **Credibility Power employs all the conventional promotional methods in a completely new wrinkle to the art of marketing. Marketing your credibility is the elevation of the individual, instead of a product or service.**

ANYONE CAN HARNESS THE POWER OF CREDIBILITY

advertising. A gullible public believed that no one would claim something that was untrue. Before government regulation, dishonest peddlers bottled colored water and people bought it as a cure-all.

Many businesses exist solely on the high praise of their patrons. For years, Coors beer was brewed only in Golden, Colorado and sold in the Rocky Mountain region. Then in the 1960s and early '70s, college students from across the country went skiing in Colorado and brought cases of the local beer back with them to dorm rooms in South Bend, Berkeley and Cambridge. Securing Coors for the next college beer bust was a major social coup. Word-of-mouth created a mystique, which created demand. And that demand pushed Coors into a full-fledged national brand.

Today, sophisticated audiences are more skeptical of paid ad claims than they were only a few years ago.

Moreover, it's harder now than in simpler times to hold people's attention long enough to make an impression with a paid advertisement. The staggering number of advertising messages pounding our eyes and ears each day forces everybody to ignore all but a tiny fraction of them. How many ads can you remember seeing or hearing in the last 24 hours? Did you act on any of them? As you are bombarded by more and more messages, you remember fewer of them.

The messages being conveyed by paid ads are diluted because of competition for the attention of readers, viewers and listeners. The only solution is to pay for more and more ads, hoping one will catch the attention of the public. While there is certainly a place for paid advertising in modern promotion, the cost of communicating a message can be prohibitive for all but the wealthiest individuals and corporations.

Public relations and conventional marketing came into practice in the 20th century as additional means of promoting products and services. We will examine the effectiveness of various promotional methods in a later chapter. All of these methods are useful in exhibiting the power of credibility.

Credibility Power is a response to skepticism about paid advertising and other forms of marketing. While advertising is all about image, credibility marketing relies heavily on information and education.

CP fills the void of trust left by increasing skepticism of paid ads and other forms of promotion.

Who Can Effectively Use Credibility Power?

Credibility Power involves bringing together knowledge on a subject and staking claim to that knowledge. One key is to utilize the available media to publicly make ourselves symbols of an area of expertise, then cash in on our position as trusted authorities in that field.

In this way, anyone with something interesting to say can use CP. Think about the last time you were at a party. Did anyone ask you what you did for a living? When an expert like Larry North talks about the specifics of fitness, he'll suggest a low-fat entrée or show how exercise can enhance the pectoral muscles. Dentists put in this position wind up gazing into mouths all night, giving advice on root canals or new ways to whiten teeth. Accountants fork over tax advice.

> The timing is right to use Credibility Power because of four especially important cultural factors:
>
> • A Media Explosion
> • The Demand for Information
> • Desktop Publishing Revolution
> • Many Potential CP Practitioners

And police officers are quizzed on city ordinances. We've all seen experts in certain fields hold the attention of those who are interested in the subject.

If we know something another person wants to know, we can use the power of credibility to gain income or respect. We don't even have to engage in a commercial enterprise to benefit. Some homeless advocates were once on the streets themselves — before they began to speak on the subject of homelessness, write books or contribute articles to local newspapers. This seemingly trivial knowledge can be very powerful.

What Factors Inspire Credibility Power?

A Media Explosion — Each time new information and entertainment media are invented, analysts predict the death of the prevailing medium. Radio was supposed to replace newspapers and books. When television became widely used, some said radio would fold. And as the Internet began to grow in the 1990s, some were convinced that all other media were doomed.

But the introduction of new media has always spurred growth in existing forms of information delivery. The same goes for new forms of old media. Because corporate mergers have reduced the ownership of large publishing houses, critics have complained that book publishing is dying. It's true that the major publishing companies are getting larger and more consolidated and are publishing fewer books. But that has caused small publishing houses to spring up all over the country to fill the void. As a consequence, more books are being published now than ever before.

As the large general interest magazines such as *Look, Life* and *The Saturday Evening Post* passed from the scene, highly specialized niche magazines filled the void with titles like *Boating, Quilting* and *Dance Spirit*. The field is so specialized that some famous people named magazines after themselves, such as *Martha Stewart's Living* and *O, The Oprah Magazine*.

When television came on line in the 1950s, radio was a collection of AM music stations. There are so many radio stations today in so many formats — talk radio, public radio, community access, foreign language and every taste in music imaginable — that stations fill the AM and FM bands and can be heard worldwide on the Internet. Some stations cover only a portion of a city, while others can be heard across the globe on the World Wide Web. There is such a demand for additional radio outlets in this country that the federal government has begun to sell licenses for low-power stations that operate in between the more powerful signals on the radio dial.

More than 100 million people are connected to the World Wide Web and 30 percent of households in the United States own a computer with Internet access. Yet the most pervasive medium in America is television. More than 90 percent of Americans own a television and about half of those are connected to cable or a satellite hookup.

An ABC television network news program, *Is America Number One?*, compared this country to others by several different measures, including what is considered to be poverty. Correspondent John Stossel claimed many items in this country that once were luxuries are now thought to be necessities. Many of the inner-city poor interviewed for this program said they owned television sets, had cable service and were linked to cyberspace. For this group, good information was deemed to be more important than good nutrition, for instance.

This craving for information is good news to people who want to enhance their position through the use of Credibility Power. People

ANYONE CAN HARNESS THE POWER OF CREDIBILITY

want to know more. And if they trust what is told to them, they will act on that information.

This media explosion can benefit the credibility marketer for a very practical reason. The more space news editors need to fill in a newspaper or time on a newscast, the more likely credibility marketers are to get space or airtime promoting ourselves. When we do a good job promoting our ideas to the marketplace, present an interesting perspective and provide solid information, some news gathering organizations will consider us worthy of mention.

The Demand for Information — As consumers today, we are bombarded with more information and advertising than we have the time and energy to evaluate. At the same time, our perceived need for information has vastly increased because of dizzying increases in products and services. The onslaught of information has increased our need to rely on trusted sources. Information that comes to us from sources we do not consider credible or trustworthy even has a name. We call it *fluff*.

We are hungry for innovative shortcuts to emerging technologies that may affect our careers. We want information in a wide variety of subject areas. We want this information well documented and evenly presented. We insist that people we trust deliver this information. Otherwise, it merely adds to our information overload rather than helping to ease it.

> For the most part, Credibility Power practitioners come from the following population groups:
>
> • **Baby Boomers**
> • **Aggressive Generation Xers**
> • **The Underemployed**
> • **The Restless Retired**

CREDIBILITY POWER

The Desktop Publishing Revolution — How can desktop publishing be important to credibility marketers? In the past two decades, desktop publishing has made the printed word faster, easier and cheaper to produce, and more available to a greater number of people. An example from our recent past tells us about the lightning-fast advancement of this technology.

As late as the 1960s, some small newspapers still printed by the hot lead method that hadn't changed much since Johannes Gutenberg perfected the use of moveable type in the 1400s.

After a story was written on a typewriter, an operator retyped it on a machine that molded hot lead into slugs of type set in columns or galleys. The process was labor- and machinery-intensive. By contrast, the paragraph you are reading was typed into a word processing program on a computer. The file was placed electronically into a layout program, fed into a film machine and converted into plates that hung on a press, and book pages resulted.

> The technology of desktop publishing makes self-publishing of books affordable for most people.

By the old method, simply getting the original story edited and rewritten often required the writer to retype the manuscript several times on a typewriter. Retyping often consumed more time than the entire desktop publishing process does today. Since time is money, the cost of setting type for a book back then often was as much as the writer's advance payment for the book. The relatively inexpensive art production methods available today enhance publishing options.

The use of technology cannot automatically make anyone a successful writer or designer of books, newsletters or brochures. But it does, at least, provide the technical ability to publish books at prices many people can afford.

Many Potential CP Practitioners — An ever-increasing number of people with resources, knowledge and interest are available to employ the CP concept.

Baby Boomers

A large proportion of our nation's business and professional leaders — members of the Baby Boom generation — are prime candidates to use the principles of Credibility Power. Born during the period from approximately 1946 to 1964, the Boomers are in their most productive work years. Many are earning income at unprecedented levels and should be enjoying the fruits of a long and productive career.

But Credibility Power is about more than making money. It's about fulfilling dreams. And many of these people are not fully utilizing their expertise due to everyday demands of job and family.

Gen-Xers

The media has portrayed the generation that followed the Baby Boom as a group of slackers with little direction. But already these people in their late 20s and 30s are beginning to emerge from the shadow of the huge Boomer generation.

The most creative and aggressive of the Gen-Xers are making names for themselves in entertainment, high-tech and a variety of youth-friendly industries. Their rise was fueled in the 1990s by the easy availability of higher education, the presumption that computerization is a young person's field and a strong economy.

These three factors have given many Gen-Xers the education, experience and financial resources needed to break out of traditional work modes. They are ripe for attempts to carve out positions of trusted authority.

The Underemployed

Talented individuals who are now unemployed or underemployed due to corporate downsizing or mergers may be attracted to the entrepreneurial aspects of Credibility Power. For those who receive severance packages or golden parachutes as they leave their former companies, there may be a sense of urgency to make things happen for themselves instead of returning to the corporate world. For those with no compensation package, there may be urgency to create income at levels they believe are unrealistic in conventional jobs.

Both of these goals are realistic by employing Credibility Power.

Restless Retired

Many retired people who've grown restless with full-time leisure may want to improve their financial future. In many cases, these are the most upbeat, energetic and financially astute members of the older generation. They have the energy and resources to pursue the position of trusted authority, the wisdom of their years and the time to make it happen.

CHAPTER 2

IN THIS CHAPTER
- CP Begins With the *Right* Expertise
- Personality Is Important
- Credibility Power at the Cutting Edge
- Strong Statements, Well Researched

Moving From Expertise to Authority

Marketable expertise, a personality that combines showmanship with persistence and the willingness to take risks can help anyone become the next big thing.

> **CREDIBILITY PROFILE**
>
> Martha Stewart's expertise extends into areas we don't even know we are interested in until she begins to talk about them. She has harnessed the power of credibility more than perhaps anyone in our culture to become an authority figure on all things domestic.

Martha Stewart knows practically everything about making a house a warm and inviting place. On television, she tells comedian Jay Leno how to create translucent handmade soaps in beautiful shapes and colors or prepare a recipe for chilled avocado soup that she discovered on a jaunt through the Yucatan.

Her larger-than-life empire — Martha Stewart Living Omnimedia, L.L.C. — went public in late 1999 and made Stewart a billionaire. Yes, that's billionaire with a "b." At that time, her holdings included:

- Two magazines — *Martha Stewart Living* and *Martha Stewart Weddings* — with a combined circulation of about 9.9 million readers each month
- More than 27 books with sales exceeding $8.5 million
- A syndicated newspaper column reaching 43 million readers each week
- A weekly segment on *CBS This Morning*
- The Emmy Award-winning *Martha Stewart Living* TV program which airs six episodes a week on affiliates of the four major networks

MOVING FROM EXPERTISE TO AUTHORITY

- A cable television program, *From Martha's Kitchen*
- A radio show five days a week on 270 stations, reaching about 1.5 million listeners
- A direct-mail catalog, *Martha by Mail*, offering 400 products
- A Web site (www.marthastewart.com) offering more than 750 products at the online *Martha by Mail* store
- Martha Stewart lines of paint, furniture and garden tools, along with bed, bath and tabletop merchandise that produced $763 million in revenue in 1998.

In an interview with Oprah Winfrey, Stewart shared her belief in the power of credibility. "I documented it (her work as a caterer) in a book called *Entertaining*, and that totally turned the tide for me, because then I became a real expert."

Her popularity is based on one highly salable idea that seems counter to common sense, but is really quite brilliant. Conventional wisdom tells us that modern women lack the time and energy necessary to present their homes in the way they would like. Stewart says they don't have time to make the bed, much less embroider a bed cover. Under this scenario, offering women realistic helpful hints only aggravates their feelings of inadequacy. Stewart gives them what have been described as "insanely elaborate, time-intensive homemaking fantasies."

> **There may be many experts in a field but fewer real authorities, whose knowledge gives them power or influence over others.**

When women can actually accomplish something Stewart suggests, they feel great. If they don't have the time or ability to do a project, that's OK, too. They simply dismiss the entire notion by saying that only Martha Stewart has the patience to accomplish something so extravagant.

In their first annual rating, the media magazine *Brill's Content* named Stewart one of the 25 most influential members of the media. In an unusual twist, the magazine's profile honored both Martha Stewart the person and Martha Stewart the brand. As the brand becomes more recognizable, the editors say, the person becomes less relevant. A sign of Stewart's success is the number of women copying her approach in publishing and on TV.

Using the principles of Credibility Power can transform a person into a brand name. Few people have used CP as effectively as Martha Stewart. Those emulating her ability to use the power of credibility can accomplish much less with it and still find success.

CP Begins with the Right Expertise

Reaching a position of trusted authority involves both expertise and marketability. An authority is well known and respected as an expert in a particular field. Authorities command influence over a large number of people within a particular relevant market because of this knowledge.

There may be many experts in a field, people with the requisite knowledge to inform others. There are fewer authorities, whose command of knowledge gives them the franchise to exert power or influence over others. How marketable that expertise is will determine the amount of influence a trusted authority will exert. The expert without marketability is simply a master of trivia. The Martha Stewart example is relevant here. Her expertise can be applied to practically every home in every developed country.

When we decide to spend our money, don't we base our actions on gathering the best information from the most reliable sources? Car buying, for example, is influenced by experience and information — how much does it cost, what are its features, how have the older models of this car performed over time?

Let's look at a car-buying decision to judge how much influence authority has over our actions.

Pursuit of just the right car might begin by viewing a television commercial or seeing a certain car on the road. We may not have a clue about the car's performance or price, but we like the way it looks with the late-day sun gleaming off its metallic torso.

That image may be enough to get us into the dealership for a test drive, but most people need more than just a car with good looks to close the deal. Other sources of information are available, and one or more of them may motivate us to buy.

Friends and acquaintances may give us the benefit of their experience with the car. These are casual sources of information with limited usefulness.

If the author of a magazine article points out that the car doesn't ride well or that it has mechanical problems, would we buy the car?

> **You must be willing to go out on a limb with fresh ideas and perspectives that are one step beyond current thinking.**

The writer of the article has become a trusted authority because of his position.

Doesn't the writer have certain credibility with us because the magazine allows him or her to express an opinion?

Personality is Important

It takes some ego involvement and a desire to be in the limelight to most effectively harness the power of credibility. The very idea that you are an expert in your field, someone who has become a trusted authority, implies that you have the persistence to make yourself stand out. The character traits of ego and persistence are important in the making of a credibility marketer.

It is important to match your personality to the correct medium used to display your expertise. A gregarious person might enjoy teaching seminars in front of masses of people or appearing on television infomercials. A shy person might resist something so public. Performing in front of the public might make you uncomfortable and unable to correctly convey information. You might be more comfortable concentrating on writing and publishing newsletters, articles or books instead.

Various surveys indicate that speaking in public is often the second greatest fear, after the fear of death itself. But under the skin of many a shy person beats the heart of a performer. It's amazing how much more relaxed you can be with practice and experience speaking before groups. Even the most confirmed shy person can do well before a group if equipped with confidence and a command of the material.

Credibility Power at the Cutting Edge

Can anyone be "the next big thing" at the cutting edge of public opinion? Increasingly, that's what the public and media are trying to discover.

When you attempt to get media outlets — television and radio stations, newspapers and magazines — to promote your rise to the position of trusted authority, remember that editors want the story other editors don't know about and, therefore, can't report. Finding out what the next big thing will be is your challenge. Martha Stewart knows women are tired of emphasizing how little time and energy they have. She has given them relief from that stale, old feeling. Larry North correctly assumes that middle-income people want the advice of a personal trainer.

Say you want to become known as the trusted authority on something like children's sports. Perhaps you sell sporting goods or work as a sports psychologist or a pediatrician. Maybe you've raised several children and want to increase awareness of the pros and cons of youth participation in sports.

Making assertions that have already been made many times before to a number of different audiences will not get you the notice you want. If you want to talk about the tendency of parents to push their children into sports, you need examples that are fresh and unusual. Few people will pay for a book or attend a seminar on a subject that has been covered before. And editors who can help promote your work will want some new slant on the subject.

Strong Statements, Well Researched

Once you define that fresh thinking and decide how far to go with it, you must be willing to deliver your message in strong, declarative statements. Often the major difference between an obscure expert and a well-known authority is the ability to simply express ideas clearly. How many times have you listened as someone in your field expressed opinions and ideas long held and understood by you? How often have you thought that you could have imparted the same information, if only you had prepared and given yourself a chance? You have more confidence in your statements if they are arrived at through research and intense preparation.

We interviewed a businesswoman who collaborated with a writer on a book about the businesswoman's work specialty. She was the reigning expert on the subject covered in the book, but when it came time to put the book together she got very busy and the writer did almost all the writing.

The businesswoman was the more outgoing and confident of the two, so when it came time to go on television, she was the main spokesperson for the book. There was only one problem. Since the writer had fleshed out most of the ideas expressed in the book, the businesswoman wasn't very familiar with them. When she went on TV, she didn't sound very sincere and had no extended remarks to make about situations described in the text.

> Few people are talented enough to "fake" their own credibility, an idea that runs contrary to the principles of credibility marketing and common sense.

Clearly, the businesswoman and the writer had a decision to make. The businesswoman was better in front of a television camera but didn't know enough about her own book. The writer knew the ideas well, but wasn't a very good conversationalist.

Did they force the writer to change his personality and become a TV star, or did they school the businesswoman on the specifics of her own book?

MOVING FROM EXPERTISE TO AUTHORITY

It was much easier and more productive to instruct the businesswoman. She proved a willing student, listening to the writer talk about the book, the examples and the research behind their conclusions. Each time the businesswoman went on television or radio or was interviewed by a newspaper, she was more confident with the material. And as the book tour progressed, the businesswoman made the book her own.

A guiding precept of Credibility Power is that you must have intimate knowledge of the ideas you present. Few people are talented enough to fake their own credibility. And even if they could, the idea of a fake authority runs contrary to the principles of both credibility marketing and common sense.

CHAPTER 3

IN THIS CHAPTER
- Earning Big Bucks from CP
- Gaining Personal Status
- Helping Others

What's the Payoff?

Credibility Power can pay off in many different ways, resulting in higher income, enhanced personal satisfaction and increased status.

WHAT'S THE PAYOFF?

> ## CREDIBILITY PROFILE
>
> Ike Vanden Eykel is one of America's top divorce lawyers. Besides increasing incomes for himself and the other lawyers in his firm, the power of credibility has given him a staging ground from which he can comment on his profession.

Ike Vanden Eykel doesn't need a pay raise. *Town & Country* magazine's "Guide to Civilized Divorce" listed him among America's top 10 divorce lawyers. Most of his clients are people of great wealth and power. With plenty to lose in a divorce, they are willing to pay Vanden Eykel to win.

He is head of the largest family law firm in the Southwest. A dozen lawyers at his firm busily help the powerful and celebrated get divorces and work out child custody arrangements.

Why would a well-to-do attorney with plenty of business promote himself and his firm? "Family law is different from other areas of the law," explains Vanden Eykel. "When you obtain a divorce for a client, he or she rarely needs your service again."

This type of attorney must generate a continual flow of business. If he stops promoting, eventually he will not be busy with the level of business that he finds challenging and financially rewarding.

Through the years, Vanden Eykel's firm has sent out brochures and announcements, run institutional advertisements and sponsored charity events. He and several of his partners have been singled out by local and state publications for their legal excellence. Vanden Eykel wanted to continue the tradition of outstanding service and take his reputation one step higher, into the realm of trusted authority. And he wanted to use that authority status to influence changes in family law.

"Too often, attorneys and their clients make the family situation worse, rather than solving problems for parents and children," he says. "I want to remind family law attorneys that they must do more than just take a client's money."

To accomplish that, Vanden Eykel worked on the concept of a less contentious divorce following a decade of emphasis on the get-even mentality.

He concluded that this milder approach is the next big thing in family law. This common-sense approach allows a family to go through the process and emerge from divorce financially and emotionally intact. There are elements of "tough love" as well as conciliation, with clients and their attorneys equally responsible for making divorce less destructive to future generations.

From this concept, Vanden Eykel authored *Successful Lone Star Divorce: How to Cope With a Family Breakup in Texas* and began his quest to become recognized not just as an expert attorney, but as a trusted authority in family law.

Earning Big Bucks from CP

There are really three ways to benefit financially from Credibility Power. You can increase the amount and quality of your core business,

WHAT'S THE PAYOFF?

create an entirely new business or realize a profit from the product of your credibility marketing venture.

For highly paid professionals like Ike Vanden Eykel, the potential income from increasing his core business far exceeds possible revenue from book sales. Most statewide books have limited sales value. By tracking the origin of his firm's business, though, Vanden Eykel is able to discern how much revenue most promotional or media relations efforts can generate for the firm.

"A profile in a local magazine keeps attracting clients to us for several years," Vanden Eykel notes. "It might generate a couple hundred thousand dollars in billings over that time. A mention in a national publication might create twice as much business."

His firm will feel the effect of *Successful Lone Star Divorce* over several years. He noticed an increase during the promotional cycle for the book. For several months, Vanden Eykel was seen on television, heard on radio and read in newspapers throughout the state. Besides benefiting from the publicity, he also uses the book as a super brochure.

"You can't believe the effect it has on potential clients when you give them a copy of your book," he says. "Most of them have consulted with four or five other attorneys beforehand, but the book clinches the deal. None of our competitors can give them something they will see on the shelves at Barnes & Noble."

An article in the 20th anniversary issue of *INC* magazine said that smart businesspeople who use books to attract large contracts view the books they write as loss leaders. The article told of one businessman who paid a ghostwriter all the money earned from the publication of his book because he understood that "his consulting business will go up $5 million a year once he has a book to leave behind on sales calls."

CREDIBILITY POWER

Case History:
Books Can Sell Faster Than Cars

When automobile dealer Carl Sewell wrote *Customers for Life* back in 1990, he was looking for a way to talk about customer service, long considered the strong point at Sewell dealerships throughout the Southwest. "I thought if the book sold 35,000 copies, it would be a great success," he told his local newspaper.

In the first four years, the book sold 500,000 copies in seven languages. The book is so popular and well read that it returns money dividends to Sewell in the following ways:

Increases in the core business — Customers are drawn to Sewell showrooms by the book, and they buy cars there because of the superior customer service Sewell describes in the book.

Creating an entirely new business — He is one of America's customer-service gurus and is paid well to speak to business groups on the subject.

Sale of the CP product — Besides individual sales, companies that rely on good customer service purchase the book in mass quantities for all their employees.

Gaining Personal Status

Even when a venture into Credibility Power does not make the practitioner rich, enhanced personal status can be a rewarding payoff. Ike Vanden Eykel is invited to participate in public forums and television roundtables on the strength of his book. He maintains that the business he receives as a consequence of these personal appearances is not as important as the prestige they provide.

Case History:
The *Bug Man* Proves Anyone Can Become A Trusted Authority

For Michael Bohdan, money is not the object. His pest control business provides him and his family with life's basic needs, and that's all the material wealth that interests him.

Bohdan wants something other than wealth. He wants respect. It's not enough for him to be the anonymous bug man who treats a person's home every three months. He wants to let people know the impact exterminators have on their lives. He wants to entertain and inform people about the power of pest control. Call it a healthy ego or the workings of a man on a mission, but he wants to place his reputation above all other pest control practitioners.

Pest controller to the stars? God's own bug man? If history has any room for famous pest-control experts, Michael Bohdan will be one.

Bohdan believes strongly that if the bug man can become a distinguished, trusted authority, anyone can accomplish that. He reached this position beginning with appearances on television and radio. He leveraged those media triumphs into the publication of a book on pest control and an instant leap over pretenders to the throne of King Cockroach.

What qualified him for such a lofty position? Bohdan spent much of his early life building up his credentials in his field. A zoology degree from Southern Illinois University began his career. He served

CREDIBILITY POWER

as a director of the Texas Pest Control Association and on the public relations committee for the National Pest Control Association. His career in the media spotlight was launched by the realization that he could have fun with all this.

In 1985, he created the World's Largest Cockroach Contest. He knew that while people are disgusted with roaches, they are also fascinated with those creatures that have been here for eons and will be here after we are gone. The World's Largest Cockroach Contest was his ticket to instant fame.

"I began to study the media and set three goals," Bohdan recalls. "I wanted to be on the *Tonight Show,* Johnny Carson's show at the time. I wanted to write a book, and I wanted my own radio show."

Bohdan began his publicity quest by watching the shows he wanted to appear on and getting a feel for the type of guests the hosts seemed to enjoy. By calling the local network affiliate stations, he obtained telephone numbers and names of producers or bookers on his target shows. Then came a round of faxes and phone calls in which Bohdan pitched himself as a guest.

He appeared on the *Tonight Show* and has photos of Johnny Carson walking a cockroach on a leash. He also did several other national and regional television shows.

When Bohdan felt he needed another promotional idea, he created the Cockroach Hall of Fame, a mini-museum located in the small store he maintains to sell pest-control items. The Hall of Fame features roaches dressed in bizarre costumes to impersonate famous peo-

WHAT'S THE PAYOFF?

ple, with names such as Roach Perot and Roachie O'Donnell.

Ideas as wacky and weird as fully clothed roaches are hard to keep secret. Through a stroke of luck, a writer doing a book called *Offbeat Museums* for a small California publisher contacted Bohdan and featured the Cockroach Hall of Fame in his book. The same company wound up publishing Bohdan's book, *What's Buggin' You?* He has appeared on local television programs in his Cockroach Dundee outfit, complete with a roach-encrusted bush hat, and he has been featured in many newspapers. His book is a top seller in its field, and he's a guest on radio programs all over the country.

As other credibility marketers have discovered, not all subject matter appeals to everyone. Bohdan was scheduled to appear on a syndicated nationwide talk show featuring comedian Dennis Miller. But the host got wind of the idea and boasted that he'd never shared the stage with a bug before and wasn't about to start.

Bohdan's love affair with cockroaches has created a publicity bonanza, but his business philosophy has prevented a monetary windfall. The way to riches in pest control is pretty simple. To handle the increased business that comes to you, you must hire people and make money off the business they service.

Most businesspeople grow their companies that way. But Bohdan has never learned to delegate. He considers his advice so important that he doesn't trust other people to deliver service as he would. And so the author of *What's Buggin' You?* is out in his pickup truck each morning, spraying for household insects and setting traps for rodents. Then each afternoon, he dispenses more advice from his pest control shop.

"It's my great failing," Bohdan admits. "I don't like to send people out to do my job, because I know they won't spend the time and do the job that I will do."

Promoting himself on national television, local radio and with his book has allowed Bohdan to become better known and appreciated. That's enough of a reward for him.

"It validates more than 20 years of work in this business," he says. "Keeping my thumb on everything allows me to remain credible to others."

He's happy to know that when you're talking bugs, your trusted authority is Michael Bohdan. He is the first to agree that if talking about bugs will make you famous, anyone can use the principles of Credibility Power to great advantage.

Helping Others

Engaging in CP to enhance your personal status can also allow you to help others. That's why religious leaders gain recognition for themselves. Dr. Billy Graham, Robert Schuller and Archbishop Desmond Tutu are examples of religious leaders who have used their high profiles to work beyond their home churches for the betterment of a larger population. In the secular world, Morris Dees, the founder and chief legal counsel for the Southern Poverty Law Center, is a good example.

Case History: From Direct Mail To a Direct Call for Justice

While a student at the University of Alabama, Morris Dees founded a direct-mail sales company that specialized in book publishing. Dees became a successful businessman who won numerous awards

WHAT'S THE PAYOFF?

from business groups. He grew Fuller & Dees Marketing Group into one of the largest publishing companies in the South. But Dees' passion was the law. The following excerpt from his autobiography, *A Season for Justice*, describes the decision he made after graduating from the University of Alabama School of Law:

"I had made up my mind. I would sell the company as soon as possible and specialize in civil rights law," Dees wrote. "All the things in my life that had brought me to this point, all the pulls and tugs of my conscience, found a singular peace. It did not matter what my neighbors would think, or the judges, the bankers or even my relatives."

Dees' business credentials were unquestioned. In 1966, the U.S. Junior Chambers of Commerce named him one of the 10 Outstanding Young Men of America. But in 1969, he sold the company to the Times Mirror Corporation, which owns *The Los Angeles Times* newspaper. Two years later, he and his law partner founded the Southern Poverty Law Center (SPLC), a nonprofit organization whose mission is to seek justice for minorities and the poor.

But Dees and the SPLC might have toiled in relative obscurity without the use of Credibility Power. Dees is known worldwide through his books and numerous pamphlets and magazines distributed by the Center to potential supporters. His autobiography was published in 1991. Two years later, he wrote *Hate on Trial: The Case Against America's Most Dangerous Neo-Nazi*. It chronicles the SPLC's lawsuit and $12.5 million judgement against white supremacist Tom

CREDIBILITY POWER

Metzger and his White Aryan Resistance for their responsibility in the beating death of a young Ethiopian student in Portland, Oregon.

Dees has been portrayed in a made-for-TV movie, *Line of Fire*, and in a feature film, *Ghost of the Mississippi*, about the life of slain civil rights worker Medgar Evers.

Fanned by the red-hot flames of Dees' celebrity, the Southern Poverty Law Center has emerged as one of the major groups that monitor extremist organizations across the country. The SPLC's strategy is to bankrupt groups that carry out specific acts and educate Americans about the need for tolerance between races, religions and socio-economic classes.

Dees devotes his time to trial work and developing ideas for Teaching Tolerance, the Center's education project.

His expertise in direct marketing has also helped the SPLC become one of the nation's most successful nonprofit groups. The Center is one of the nonprofit world's most aggressive direct mail solicitors.

Contributors and potential supporters of the Center receive magazines and booklets that trumpet the successes of Dees and his organization on a monthly basis and as the legal staff of the SPLC makes courtroom history. At a time when many nonprofits are struggling to define their mission and remain viable, the SPLC has been able to build a new headquarters building (after the old facility was firebombed) in Montgomery, Alabama, complete with a memorial to victims of the civil rights struggle. The Center is now working to build an endowment to secure the financial stability of the organization for many years to come.

Dees' critics claim that he is merely a publicity hound who is getting rich off donations from gullible people all across the country. Those comments show that his use of Credibility Power, along with an aggressive direct mail campaign, has been roundly successful.

Anyone Can Benefit From Credibility Power

The types of vocations that benefit from CP are as varied as the choices people make in their lives. Our research has encountered Credibility Power in the following areas of work (in alphabetical order):

Academics	Journalism
Construction	Law
Cooking	Marketing
Corporate	Military
Credit Advisory	Medical
Financial Services	Motivation
Gardening	Nonprofits
Health and Fitness	Pest Control
High-Tech	Politics
Home Improvement	Real Estate
Home Repair	Religion
Human Resources	Retailing
Insurance	Sales
Internet	

Those who utilize Credibility Power often follow a fairly predictable path. They do something long enough to become very good at it. They make a conscious decision to become better known in a certain field. They produce a product or service that gains the attention of the media and the public. Then they benefit through increased income, enhanced prestige or helping others.

CHAPTER 4

IN THIS CHAPTER
- Model 1 — The Evolutionary Expert
- Model 2 — The Accidental Expert
- Model 3 — Professional on the Prowl
- Model 4 — Celebrity Appeal
- Model 5 — The Inevitable Expert

Credibility Role Models: Learning from the Best

Experts who utilize the power of credibility can be classified into five distinct models determined by the unique ways they reached authority status.

CREDIBILITY ROLE MODELS

> **CREDIBILITY PROFILE**
>
> Dottie Walters has used the power of credibility to grow from a small-town ad salesperson into an internationally known motivational speaker. Her books, seminars and newsmagazine prove that persistence pays off.

Dottie Walters is one of the heroes of CP who earned the position of trusted authority in an unusual way. World War II had just ended. Her husband had returned from the war and they had bought a house in a small town in Southern California when a deep recession hit.

Walters needed to work, but what could she do? She only had a high school education. She didn't own a car and she had two small children. Her only experience remotely similar to working was as feature editor and advertising manager of her high school newspaper. But when Walters approached the local newspaper publisher, he said he didn't need help.

That told Walters the newspaper didn't have enough advertising customers. So she became one. She bought ad space at a wholesale rate, sold it at retail and pocketed the difference. These ads took the form of a column Walters wrote about shopping in the various stores in town. Her problem was getting herself and her product in front of local merchants.

"I would go walk and walk, and I had cardboard in my shoes," Dottie remembers. "I was pushing my two babies in a stroller and the wheels kept coming off. And I noticed the merchants were not in their

CREDIBILITY POWER

stores. Then I saw in the newspaper that the Kiwanis Club and the Rotary and the Lions Club were all having their meetings. That's where the merchants were. They were at those meetings and each meeting had a speaker. What if I could be that speaker? I could speak to a roomful of prospects, rather than walking all over town looking for them.

"I talked about what customers want," she says. "I laid my newspapers with my column in front of each luncheon plate, picked up their business cards and had a little drawing. I gave away a ballpoint pen, which was gift-wrapped. And I took their cards home and sold the advertising over the phone. They took my calls and bought ads because they had seen my column and knew who I was from my speaking."

Walters found out that even though she was a woman talking to men's clubs, every group wanted to hear her. It wasn't that she wanted to get up in front of people and speak. She just wanted to present her product before a lot of potential buyers. They didn't give her money for speaking, but she was well paid.

"I got paid in customers," she says. "It was much easier than trying to walk. I could be home with my children."

She set up her dining room as an office with orange crates she hauled home from the grocery store and a typewriter she borrowed from a friend. Her method worked because she did what she said she would do and because she was creative with the ads.

CREDIBILITY ROLE MODELS

From this humble beginning, the merchants convinced Walters that she should open an advertising company. She called it Hospitality Hostess.

"Through the merchants' help, I opened it and went from town to town," she says. "Because I spoke to service clubs all over, within two years I grew that company up to 285 employees and 4,000 continuous contract advertising accounts in four offices around Southern California."

As her business grew, Walters conducted seminars and workshops to teach her own employees how to sell advertising. She was asked to speak on the subject to groups all over the state. She began to get paid for her talks and received invitations to address sales groups across the country and even outside the United States.

"I wrote the first book for women in sales," she says. "It is called *Never Underestimate the Selling Power of A Woman*. My timing was perfect. All the big companies starting up, like Tupperware and Amway, wanted women to work for them. They called me and I toured the United States and Canada and England speaking to women going into sales. I talked about how women can sell and why we're good at it."

Many of the groups she spoke to had so much confidence in her ability that they began to ask her about other speakers. "They said, 'Dottie that was wonderful. Now, next time we want a comedian. Or next time we want somebody on this subject or that subject. Would you help us?' So I began to recommend my friends. And then the thought came to me — Dottie, why don't you start a speaker's bureau?"

Today, Walters is president of Walters Speakers Services. Besides filling her own speaking engagements throughout the world, she hosts a regular radio program for National Business Radio Network that's

CREDIBILITY POWER

heard in 75 major American cities. She is publisher of SHARING IDEAS, an international newsmagazine for the paid speaking field. She writes for publications all over the world and does interviews with the television networks as well as radio broadcasts heard on United Airlines and Delta Air Lines flights. She is a founding member of the National Speakers Association and the International Group of Agencies and Bureaus.

Her company sells books, video and audiotapes and software for people who want to become paid speakers. *Never Underestimate the Selling Power of a Woman* (1986) is in its 15th edition. And she has written two other books: *Speak and Grow Rich* (1989) and *101 Simple Things to Grow Your Business* (1995).

One of the children she pushed from store to store in that stroller was her daughter. Lilly Walters is now executive director of Walters International Speakers Bureau, a subsidiary of Walters Speakers Services that represents 30,000 presenters, from celebrities to business speakers. Lilly was co-author of *Speak and Grow Rich*. The Walters team sends speakers all over the world for such companies as Shell Oil, Lockheed Martin, Litton, IBM, McDonnell Douglas and AT&T.

The journey of Dottie Walters from unemployed housewife to internationally known sales and motivational speaker is no overnight success story. It took more than 25 years to reach her level of success, which involved dynamic use of Credibility Power principles from those initial speeches to her career as an international speaker. But knowing how she started and how improbable her ascendancy was, it could be said that Walters originated her own personal Credibility Power model.

How did she accomplish everything? Because she couldn't afford to fail. Looking back on her struggle, though, Walters sees herself mostly as a crusader for the rights of women in the sales workplace.

CREDIBILITY ROLE MODELS

"I got such a vision with that first book," she says. "When women in sales picked up a book by a man and it suggested you pass out cigars, we knew we'd been left out. They weren't talking about us. And so I felt all of these women standing behind me, and I needed to help them."

Her vision compelled her to continue until she was a success using the power of credibility. To be successful, you must envision success down the line. Vision is the constant companion of our credibility role models.

model 1
THE EVOLUTIONARY EXPERT:
From Government Employee to Gardening Superstar

Neil Sperry evolved from a government agricultural agent into one of the nation's top horticultural entrepreneurs. He did it with a love of gardening and a compulsion to always tell the truth.

Few people have written a bible. Neil Sperry is one of them. *Neil Sperry's Complete Guide to Texas Gardening* is on the coffee table of gardeners all over the state. The guy palpably oozes credibility. You don't plant a petunia or prune a plum tree in the Lone Star State without first checking with Sperry. In this way, he is an extraordinary example of the power of credibility.

Sperry is the role model for many practitioners of CP. He is the guy who has held the same job for a number of years. It's a job he enjoys. He does it well, and that allows him to move into ventures that can propel him above the other people in his field.

The masses of working people rarely launch into other ventures. They hesitate because of feelings of insecurity. But those who take the plunge are the experts who evolve into trusted authorities.

Sperry has the black dirt of Texas in his blood. His parents worked at the state's agricultural college, his father as a professor and his mother as a staff member. Sperry left the state in 1964 to earn two degrees from Ohio State University and teach horticulture in an Ohio high school.

He returned to Texas as a County Extension horticulturist. For almost eight years, he served 17 counties. It was satisfying work with only one drawback.

"I just got tired of giving programs every night of the week for seven months of the year and never seeing my family," Sperry says. "I did some television, radio and writing for the newspaper as part of my job. And I really enjoyed that. At that point, there was no one in Texas who was doing garden broadcasting."

Sperry befriended the host of a radio program about do-it-yourself home repair, then did guest spots on his friend's show. Station management saw their ratings increase when Sperry was on the air, so they asked him to host his own show in 1978.

Many of the people doing garden broadcasting in other states were more concerned with selling the products sponsoring their shows than giving good advice. Sperry's idea was revolutionary for the time. He thought a gardening product he endorsed should do a good job for the people who ultimately paid the bills — his listeners. He was working for them, not the sponsors. He figured people would listen to him only if he had personal credibility. Sperry was actually marketing his own credibility as a master gardener.

CREDIBILITY ROLE MODELS

This common-sense approach got him into trouble at the radio station, but it certainly made his career more successful over the long term. One day the station manager wanted him to endorse a soil additive, which is illegal in most states. "Texas does not have a law against it," he explains. "I can grind up this telephone and sell it to you in a bag as a soil amendment, and I don't have to prove that it is or isn't beneficial."

Sperry gave management an ultimatum. Either choose soil additives or him. They sided with their sponsor. Sperry joined another local news station in 1980 and has been there ever since.

He wrote the gardening bible in 1982. *Neil Sperry's Complete Guide to Texas Gardening* has been through more than 50 printings and has sold more than 500,000 copies. It is now the fourth best-selling hardback gardening book in the nation.

"I knew Texas needed a gardening book," Sperry says. "I was getting all my information for the radio show from books about other states and having to interpret what they meant to Texas."

Sperry began a tabloid publication that is inserted into the local newspaper each week in the spring. He put out his first gardening calendar soon after publishing his book. Then in the mid-1980s, he began to publish a monthly magazine called *Neil Sperry's Gardens*.

In 1997, he published his second book, *1001 Most Asked Texas Gardening Questions*. Now he does an hour-long program on the statewide radio network and syndicates a weekly gardening column in 20 Texas newspapers.

With some of his ventures, Sperry took on investors or partners. But he bought them out after a while. "That way I can do things the way I think they should be done," he notes. "When I take on a project, either I try to find the people who can make it really great, like a good cameraman or a good editor, or I try to do that part myself."

CREDIBILITY POWER

Over more than 20 years, Sperry has had plenty of opportunities to sell out and betray his public. But he's too smart for that. He has evolved from government employee to gardening superstar.

The American Association of Nurserymen has named him the Garden Communicator of the Year. The Texas Agricultural Extension Service named Sperry Man of the Year in Agriculture. And he is the winner of five top national awards from the Garden Writers Association of America.

Of the many regional gardening experts in the country, Sperry is probably the most secure in his position. You would expect nothing less from the man who wrote the bible.

CREDIBILITY ROLE MODELS

model 2
THE ACCIDENTAL EXPERT:
Using The Power to Create Celebrity

When Oprah Winfrey asked him how to repair her life, Dr. Phillip McGraw didn't try to placate her. He dealt with her in a blunt, "tell it like it is" style. The rest is an object lesson in the power of credibility.

Dr. Phillip McGraw was a little-known forensic psychologist with a decent reputation and a limited practice before 1998. His specialty is what those in his business call trial science. He helps attorneys and their clients select the most favorable people to serve on their juries. His company, Courtroom Sciences, Inc., assists in all phases of trial preparation, from conducting research with mock trials to a complete array of courtroom graphics and computer animation.

McGraw, a tall, imposing figure and a former athlete, is a prime example of the two levels of fame that result from Credibility Power. At the top end, there is universal fame. This is the Tom Hanks, Michael Jordan, Peter Jennings variety. It is an extraordinary level of notice. Everywhere they go, people know their names and faces. They can't sit down in restaurants without people asking, "Aren't you so-and-so?" Sometimes with actors, they become the characters they portray on television or in the movies. Universal fame just happens to a person when he or she isn't looking.

The other fame is specific and targeted. A person can actually work toward this kind of fame, and it's more manageable. The more specific kind of fame is within an industry or other subset of the population. People at this level of fame barely cause a blip on the screen of recognition among the general public. But they are famous within their business or social group.

McGraw has now experienced both kinds of fame. He has worked on some of the largest civil court cases of the past decade. His clients include *Fortune 500* companies, major airlines and media personalities. His company also worked on the legal case arising from the Exxon Valdez oil spill in Alaska.

But few people in the general public knew his face or name until he went to work for talk show host Oprah Winfrey in 1998. He was hired when Oprah's television production company was sued by a group of cattlemen for supposedly defaming beef products. McGraw and his company helped select the jury in this case. And he wound up serving as Winfrey's unofficial therapist.

Newspaper accounts tell the story of the talk show host's struggle with what she saw as a vicious and unfair attack against her. She thought she was just doing her job when she had an animal rights advocate on her show. Who'd have thought that comments about eating beef could get her sued?

Her distress was so intense that she sought out McGraw's advice during an especially difficult time in a trial that could cost her and her company millions if they lost.

McGraw told Winfrey she had a choice to make. She could continue to live in denial and resist what was happening to her because she didn't like it, or she could understand that she was in a war and fight back. At McGraw's urging, Winfrey fought back and the jury verdict came back in her favor.

From that conversation, and others like it during the trial, came the making of Dr. Phil, Media Celebrity. He wrote a book, which was touted on *The Oprah Winfrey Show*, called *Life Strategies: Doing What Works, Doing What Matters*. The book reached No. 1 on *The New York*

CREDIBILITY ROLE MODELS

Times bestseller list. In the first three months, it sold more than half a million copies.

Oprah gave him the nickname Dr. "Tell It Like It Is" Phil, and he became a regular guest on her show. His honest, forthright style — confronting people without seeming to bully them — makes him a perfect fit as one of her "Change Your Life TV" experts.

Interviewed by a local newspaper, *The Dallas Observer*, McGraw says he was terrified the first time he was on the show. "For what I do, it's like a free fall," he was quoted as saying. "There's a guy on his back with a camera down here, and there's a boom mike coming over the top of you here, and there's some guy counting down to break over there, and you're trying to have an intimate moment with someone."

His fellow psychologists — who both like and envy him very much — are amazed at McGraw's ability to promote himself. They claim he doesn't have anything new or different to say.

What McGraw does is listen very intently to the questions and comments of those he is there to help, then he replies to them in a simple, direct style. His method is designed to cause them to examine their own lives and figure out for themselves what will make things better.

He doesn't use jargon. He doesn't qualify his statements in ways that cloud the simplicity of his message. He understands the limitations of television and how much of himself to reveal to the camera and the audience.

> **Dr. Phil's simple, direct style plays well on national TV, making the most of his friendship with talk show host Oprah Winfrey.**

Equally important to his success, though, is that he quite by accident befriended one of the most powerful women in America. When Oprah Winfrey says you are OK, you are just that to millions of television watchers. Oprah's Book Club is proof of that point. Between mid-1996 and mid-1999, Winfrey selected 26 books for her viewers to read and analyze. Twenty-five of these books zoomed onto *USA Today's* bestseller list, with the one exception already on the list before it was chosen. Oprah-certified books account for 11 percent of Barnes & Noble's entire sales of fiction titles.

Winfrey's power to create celebrity is overwhelming, and she successfully transferred some of her credibility to "Dr. Phil." He was given his own address on the show, so that people can write in for advice on matters involving themselves and their loved ones. His second book, *Relationship Rescue*, pushed its way up the charts after several mentions on the show. And a third book indicates an increasingly narrow focus on the same subject matter. Written with his son, it deals with the relationship problems of teenagers.

The Accidental Expert has evolved into someone who draws crowds in his own right. He conducts seminars on relationships all across the country and does guest spots on other television and radio programs. The key for him is when the opportunity presented itself, McGraw was ready for the challenge. He didn't tell himself the reasons he couldn't take advantage of his encounter with celebrity. He followed what he presents as Life Law No.1: Either you get it or you don't.

Dr. Phillip McGraw has plugged into Credibility Power in a very big way.

CREDIBILITY ROLE MODELS

model 3

PROFESSIONAL ON THE PROWL:
An Expert Who Was Meant to Be

Tom Hopkins made his fortune in real estate at age 20. Then he set out to become the very best teacher of sales techniques in the world. Ask any of his students and they'll tell you — he has reached his goal.

Hopkins didn't just happen into sales training as his life's work. After retiring from real estate sales at the ripe old age of 27, he was on the prowl for a new and challenging career. If Dr. Phillip McGraw is an Accidental Expert, Hopkins is the Intentional Expert who has become America's trusted authority in the area of sales training and motivation.

Hopkins likes to describe his rise from "a $42-a-month failure" to millionaire. He attended college for less than a semester, then did construction work. He went into real estate, and in six months he made almost nothing. That was back in 1964. Then something happened that he also likes to describe:

"I loved the field of selling and what I was selling was real estate," Hopkins recalls. "I began to work day and night, I loved it so. After eight years I had sold more homes than anyone had ever sold. That earned me a reputation, and people invited me to speak to their groups. I found that I could teach others. And as far as being an expert at speaking and teaching, having done thousands of seminars, if you do something enough, you become pretty good at it."

Hopkins taught himself how to sell real estate and built his sales volume to more than $14 million in five years.

"Real estate was a middle-aged man's business back in the '60s," he says. "That made me something of an oddity. The California Association of Realtors asked me to speak to them on how I could do so well by the time I was 20."

His ability to simplify complex emotional experiences is at the root of his success in sales training. A good example is his explanation of how to become an expert:

"I have three little words — practice, drill and rehearse so that you sound like an expert, do a better job than anybody else and the world will beat a path to your door."

What is his philosophy of how to excel at work? "You have to fall in love with your job because then it's not work," he says. "It's something you can't wait to do. Treat it like a hobby. If everyone treated a job like that, they would love to do it, talk about it, read books about it, become great at it."

Hopkins was able to look at his new job teaching sales techniques from this perspective because he was financially secure. "I didn't have to make money," he says. "That's when you really can do something creative."

He purchased a sales training school in Phoenix and founded Tom Hopkins International, Inc. (THI) in 1976. Since then, he has trained more than 3 million salespeople on five continents. Hopkins personally conducts 75 seminars each year traveling throughout the United States, Canada, Australia, New Zealand and the Far East. His graduates or champions, learn to increase both their selling skills and sales volumes by listening to Hopkins and his staff.

CREDIBILITY ROLE MODELS

Once each year, Hopkins hosts a three-day sales boot camp near his headquarters in Scottsdale, Arizona. This program is designed for "the world's highest-paid sales professionals" to undergo intensive training in selling skills and overall career enhancement.

While Hopkins and assorted guest speakers are holding forth at the front of the room during his seminars, there is usually brisk business going on in the back.

Hopkins is a master of back-of-the-room sales, with 10 books and an assortment of audiocassette tapes produced over the past decade. His book, *How to Master the Art of Selling*, has sold more than 1.3 million copies worldwide and has been translated into 10 languages.

Recently, Hopkins authored two books in the "…for Dummies" series for IDG Books Worldwide. *Sales Closing for Dummies* and *Sales Prospecting for Dummies* are top sellers at seminars and on bookstore shelves.

Wherever Hopkins goes, he runs into people who've become successful through his words. "The greatest reward for a teacher is for students to go out and do the job," he says. "I love the teaching. I love the helping and love it when people come back and tell me they've doubled and tripled their incomes. That's really what I call payment to a teacher."

For Hopkins, there are very few challenges today that he has not met. He is a charter member of the National Speakers Association and was among the first to receive the group's Council of Peers Award for Excellence.

"I've just been very blessed," he says. "Everything is going so well. I have a wonderful staff that travels with me. And I've got a wonderful wife and great kids and grandkids. I mean, it's just super."

Tom Hopkins intended it all to happen this way.

CREDIBILITY POWER

model 4

CELEBRITY APPEAL:
His Name is Still Golden After All These Years

One day you're risking everything to reach your goal. The next day you succeed at it and have to set a new goal and find a completely new pathway to success. What do you do? Bruce Jenner has successfully used the principles of Credibility Power to answer that question for more than two decades.

The lives of world-class athletes after their heyday are much different from regular folks. Athletes who own an Olympic gold medal, a Super Bowl ring or the famed green jacket from the Masters golf tournament can live off the good old days if they choose.

People pay to appear on the golf course and walk 18 holes with these athletes. Everywhere celebrities eat or drink, fans from the glory days will pick up the tab. These athletes may not have assets themselves, but they don't need many. They can live off adoring fans who remember their name.

But Bruce Jenner didn't want to rest on his laurels after winning the gold medal in the decathlon in the 1976 Summer Olympics. At age 26, he wasn't ready to retire. But he wasn't sure what he would do.

"I started out as a guy who was so enriched by what he was doing and trying to win the Games that I really didn't have an opportunity to expand myself," he says. "The life of an athlete who's trying to become the best in the world at something doesn't lead you into other areas. I didn't have other interests. All my motivation, interest, time, energy and dreams went into fulfilling one big dream. But I competed in the Games in 1976 and I was retired from athletics the next day."

Today, athletes of Jenner's stature sign contracts that ensure their livelihood before they compete. But this was more than two decades ago. Olympians were true amateurs in every sense of the word. The thought of making money off an Olympic performance was suspect. It took Jenner a few days to see the potential for cashing in on his new fame and an acceptable way to proceed.

"Television has such an enormous impact," Jenner notes. "I was fortunate that ABC Sports latched on to my story. I was so preoccupied running around the track doing my thing that I didn't know what the world was seeing until after the competition and realized that, hey, things had changed drastically."

Two weeks before the Olympic Games in Montreal, Jenner was in New York City and nobody noticed him. Two days after he captured the decathlon gold medal and set a world record, he was back in New York. He couldn't walk down the street because of the crowds who mobbed him.

"I happened to be the right guy in the right place at the right time," Jenner remembers. "Now it was my job to figure out what I wanted to do with the opportunities at hand. Where do I want to be five, 10 or 20 years down the line? My first feeling was that I did not want to do anything that would tarnish my performance. Keep everything highly credible and don't do too many things just for money. You know, you can make a lot of money really fast but then people say that you're only in it for the money and they don't like you because you're getting really greedy."

In his quest to construct a new life, Jenner accepted a five-year deal from General Mills to be on a Wheaties box. Then he became a sportscaster with ABC Sports.

CREDIBILITY POWER

"Right from the get-go, I didn't think I was this big name and didn't have to work at it," he says. "I knew that I had four years to get my education in TV sports. Come the next Summer Olympics, if I'm not good at what I do and don't learn the business side of television, when the next name comes along he would get my job."

Although he was known around the world, Jenner came in with an attitude that would benefit anyone who utilizes Credibility Power. Never burn any bridges. Don't come in with the big head. Remember people's names. Write thank-you notes to people who help you. Always be professional.

In return for this caring attitude, television has been good to Jenner. He served as a guest host and correspondent for *Good Morning America*. He covered every Olympics through the 1992 Barcelona Games. He appeared as a guest on several prime-time network shows. He branched out into movies and did infomercials for exercise equipment. He founded his own production company and produced several made-for-TV movies and a 26-segment health show.

> **Bruce Jenner went into this post-Olympics career with the correct attitude. Remember people's names. Write thank you notes to those who help you. Always be professional.**

Today, Jenner is highly prized as a commercial spokesman for such major companies as Ford, VISA, Coca-Cola, Minolta and Firestone. He enjoys speaking at sales meetings or representing these companies and their products in advertising. He is also hired to give motivational speeches at seminars for corporations and individual businesspeople all across the country.

Wherever he goes, people still remember the muscular young American waving the Stars and Stripes after winning the decathlon to become known as "the World's Greatest Athlete."

His motivational talks concern how to compete successfully in life and business. He turned that message into a book, *Finding the Champion Within* (1996). He has also published *Bruce Jenner's Viewers' Guide to the Olympics* and *A Teenage Guide to Fitness*.

Jenner has also felt the personal affronts suffered by people who put themselves in the spotlight. He and his first wife went through a much-publicized divorce. He was almost broken financially and held himself together only by working harder at his job of being Bruce Jenner.

Now, though, Jenner is leading a good life. Most of his working time is spent giving motivational speeches and attending to corporate matters. When he's not on the road, he is at home in Los Angeles with his second wife, Kris, and their children.

A newspaper story on Jenner summed up his life this way: "Since his retirement from track, Jenner has been busier than an army of ants. He has raced cars, powerboats and mountain bikes. He has piloted his own jet plane. He has been a sports broadcaster, producer, promoter, actor and author. He has been a guest host on *Good Morning America*. He has put out his own line of fitness products."

When asked to tell what made him a success, Jenner is quick to say that it was his childhood battle with dyslexia. When he tried to read, words became jumbled and sentences short-circuited. He believes that most people who achieve something great have had to overcome some obstacle.

"If it wasn't for dyslexia, I don't think I ever would have been an

Olympic champion," he reflects. "Sports became my arena, and I worked hard to prove myself."

And what has proven to be most important to his success after sports? "My name — it's golden, even after all these years," he says. "My name is my business. The basic thing is my personal credibility in my name and what I do. When you own something that valuable, you have to protect it."

model 5
THE INEVITABLE EXPERT:
Being in the Right Place at the Right Time

Colin Powell and Norman Schwarzkopf served their country well. It was inevitable that history — and the American people — would reward them.

Military figures have a special place in the hearts of Americans. We have elected six military heroes as president in our nation's history. Dwight Eisenhower was so popular after leading the Allied armies in World War II that both political parties wanted him to be their nominee. Today, we put former military leaders on television, read their books and pay them to inspire us with their speeches.

During the Persian Gulf War, news organizations hired many retired generals or admirals to provide expert commentary on our conflict with Iraq and its possible implications. The long buildup to the war, and the resulting battles, provided a showcase for their talents that has kept many of these military people employed even today as security analysts. In terms of Credibility Power, it is the maximum use of an inevitable ride to success.

Some of these military leaders have used their positions to publicize very worthwhile charitable or philanthropic efforts. They were in the right place at the right time. Something greater than them personally (a war, for instance), propelled them into the seat of authority, and they made the most of it. To our way of thinking, their journey to success is the best example of realizing the American dream.

CREDIBILITY POWER

Two of our most Inevitable Experts are retired U.S. commanders Colin Powell and Norman Schwarzkopf. They have followed similar paths to success following their Desert Storm adventure.

Powell is the most public of the two figures, since he has been touted as a possible presidential or vice presidential candidate and has served in high-level government positions since retiring from the Army following the war.

Powell wrote a best-selling book, *My American Journey*. He helped found the nationwide volunteer group America's Promise, which is dedicated to assisting in the education and development of children. He has taken positions on corporate boards and was a much sought after speaker before becoming Secretary of State in the administration of President George W. Bush. Powell's speaking fees often topped $50,000 and his personal appearances have brought rave reviews for his message and speaking style. He remains perhaps the most respected figure in American life today.

Schwarzkopf, too, wrote a bestseller, *It Doesn't Take a Hero*. He is a spokesman for STARBRIGHT Foundation, an organization formed to improve the quality of life for children with serious illnesses. He is also a spokesman for prostate cancer awareness, and he appears on a circuit with other motivational speakers such as Tom Hopkins and Zig Ziglar.

Powell and Schwarzkopf have leveraged their positions as national heroes into success using Credibility Power. But people other than military heroes can jump on the gravy train. We all can profit from understanding how important or interesting our experiences are to others.

People who've gone through a corporate merger or downsizing can become experts on flourishing during difficult times. Workers in a given industry can become trusted authorities on procedures inside

CREDIBILITY ROLE MODELS

that industry. Those who have worked in government may have had experiences that would interest other people. Writing articles and books, speaking to groups or giving radio and television interviews are important ways to communicate life experiences.

CHAPTER 5

IN THIS CHAPTER
- Key #1 — Overcoming Obstacles
- Key #2 — The Importance of Desire
- Key #3 — Getting There First
- Key #4 — Researching the Product
- Key #5 — Focusing Your Effort

Five Keys to Developing Expertise Into a Marketable Asset

To successfully harness Credibility Power, your expertise must be valuable in the marketplace. This chapter includes five key elements that make your knowledge more marketable.

FIVE KEYS TO DEVELOPING EXPERTISE

> **CREDIBILITY PROFILE**
>
> Bob Bauer was satisfied living the scientist's life closeted in his research lab. But with his company's new emphasis on the scientist as communicator, he spends a significant amount of his working time selling his lab's ability to people both inside and outside the corporation.

Who would have thought that science geeks would become the rock stars of the new economy? Bob Bauer never had a clue back in the 1970s, as he toiled away as a lab manager at Xerox Corporation's Palo Alto (California) Research Center, known in scientific circles by its acronym, PARC.

The Ph.D. physicist with a bachelor's degree in electrical engineering was happy in the laboratory that has contributed to many of this century's technological innovations, such as lasers and personal computers. PARC scientists have helped spawn such innovative companies as Apple Computer and Adobe Systems International.

In Bauer's early days at PARC, the only public displays of his credibility appeared in professional and academic publications. His research resulted in more than 100 journal articles and 10 books on technical subjects. Like most high-tech companies of the day, Xerox operated under an old-fashioned model. Scientists didn't cater to the needs of customers. They stayed sequestered in their labs while the salespeople presented their inventions to the public.

"That all changed in the early 1990s," Bauer says. "Competition intensified to attract lead customers. People inside the company realized the great investment we have in research and began to understand how those of us who created the solutions to problems can assist sales and marketing."

This new understanding called for a unique transformation by the company's scientific work force. Scientists and other research workers are now part of the sizzle as well as the steak in many industrial companies. They might not have welcomed it at first, but Bauer says this major paradigm shift has made his work life richer and more varied.

Scientist Bob Bauer steps out of the corporate laboratory and into the sales environment.

Like many of his fellow scientists, he attends conferences and meetings all over the world. Along with the center director and many of the research staff, Bauer participates at industry events, media relations activities and an executive briefing program. PARC also hosts 80 to 100 visits each year by major customer groups. These visits generally involve a tour or overview, plus talks and conversations with the people involved in research projects. Managers are asked to expound on their vision of the future, a look at science and technology that most sales and marketing people can't adequately explain.

"Instead of just sitting in our labs developing products," Bauer says, "we go out to meet our customers, find out the problems they have and how best to solve them. That's how new products come about today."

Xerox has a worldwide presence and many thousands of employees, and Bauer says one of his most important jobs is informing people inside the company about the capabilities of PARC.

"It was decided that PARC would not simply respond to company needs, but would take an active role in corporate marketing and strategy," he explains.

With the increasing interest in what scientists have to say, Bauer has taken on many public relations duties. Whenever he speaks at a conference, there are often newspaper and television interviews that accompany his main talk. He has contributed to national and international magazine articles. And he prepared talks on several topics when Xerox bought time on a business network that broadcasts through the sound system on transcontinental airline flights.

Research and development is a great expense to the corporation. The measures undertaken by Bauer are designed to bring science geeks in closer proximity to what really matters in the corporate world — producing revenue. "It's hard to quantify what our efforts mean to the success of the company," he says, although in the next breath he recalls a talk he gave at a conference in Hawaii that convinced a large, reluctant customer to cast his lot with Xerox.

PR manager Jennifer Ernst says the involvement of science professionals has the most influence at two key points in the sales cycle. "The first is when an account manager is working to get a potential customer to give Xerox serious consideration in a bidding process," she says. "The credibility and vision of PARC people has often been credited with giving Xerox an opportunity to participate, often resulting in revenue generation."

The other crucial point is when a customer is close to the decision point on a major purchase. Backup by scientists like Bauer often makes the difference.

"One highly successful direct marketing campaign featured an essay series by the Xerox chief scientist," Ernst says. "It was credited with generating more than $150 million in revenue, as of some time in 1999."

Bauer acknowledges that this new approach to the job of scientist and corporate manager has greatly increased his credibility in the marketplace of ideas. He recommends such efforts to anyone within a corporation who wants additional challenges. He says the expanded public role rounds out the image of those in his field who "tend to be insecure, although people who aren't scientists think we're all arrogant."

But what rock star doesn't display a little arrogance?

Here are five keys to developing your expertise into a marketable asset:

Key #1: Overcoming Obstacles

Practitioners of Credibility Power have many obstacles to overcome in reaching goals. Larry North had to deal with a difficult childhood. Dottie Walters' lack of education, money and experience hindered her. Bruce Jenner dealt with dyslexia as a kid.

Each of these individuals turned a deficit into a plus. North and Walters have made their most obvious handicaps part of their résumés. Their job is to inspire others to superior performance, and they offer themselves as examples of the ability to overcome problems and reach success.

For Jenner, having dyslexia is one of the most important stories he tells to inspire people. This condition was originally used to focus his own energies. Because he was dyslexic, school work was difficult. He was embarrassed to have the teacher call on him. In sports, he could excel without having to read aloud.

Many of us believe we face insurmountable obstacles. Some of these obstacles are real, like learning problems, poverty or abuse. Frankly, we construct others so that we don't have to get out into the world and expose ourselves to the possibility of failure.

Consider the obstacles to writing. People who write for a living regularly hear people tell them about how they've always wanted to write. What's stopping anyone from writing? It requires fewer qualifications, genetic preconditioning and equipment than almost any other discipline. A college degree isn't required. Family connections are not necessary. Neither a computer nor a word processor is essential. A pencil and pad of paper will do. Writing only requires an idea, a certain amount of organization and the persistence to spend many hours alone. Good writing may be difficult to achieve, but it only happens after a person sits down to write and rewrite and rewrite.

The first key to producing a marketable asset is actually getting something done. And each of us must evaluate whether the obstacles we face are real or self-manufactured.

Case History: Sports and the Gift of Gab

The Leon Simon phenomenon could have taken place in any large American city where sports is big business. Simon is possible because millions of us talk incessantly about sports. It is the closest most of us ever come to a relationship with our sports heroes.

Simon can talk sports. He's done it for years as a football coach for young kids and as a barber at the "Nice Looks" barbershop. Sports opinions fly in predominantly African-American barber shops, and most of those opinions deal with which defensive back got traded, why the cleanup hitter was sent out there to bunt and what's wrong with the local pro basketball team's power forward.

"I used to call into the talk shows a lot," Simon recalls, "and they seemed to think I knew what I was talking about."

CREDIBILITY POWER

He became "Leon in Oak Cliff," a regular call-in contributor to the radio sports scene. When the ratings for one sports show began to drop on the weekends, the station manager asked Simon to help boost ratings for a Sunday afternoon show.

"I never applied for it," Simon recalls. "I didn't think I had the right background to get anything like that. Of course, I'm not saying I didn't want it, but I never thought I could get it. They just offered me the job."

Simon was truthful with station management. He didn't know a thing about radio, but that didn't seem to matter. "They said, 'All we want you to do is be Leon. If you don't know an answer, just say so.' You know, I can do that. I did that every day at the barber shop."

He handled the Sunday show for two years and continued to cut hair during the week. Then he switched to the evening show during the week, and he cut hair in the mornings.

His increasing prominence on the radio gave his haircutting business a boost, but not as much as he thought it would. Simon was always the sidekick, a commentator reacting to the leading comments of his co-host, who was a longtime radio veteran. This format rarely allowed him to direct the on-air conversation to such topics as where the listener could get a good haircut. Any mention of his career off the radio was purely accidental.

After a while, Simon was shifted to the station's top-rated program, a sports show in morning drive time. This move put an end to his work as a barber, but he developed into one of the best-known radio personalities in the area.

To Simon, it is a career he enjoyed. But he was not passionate about it. "If the ratings go down or the station changes, I can always go back to cutting hair," he once said.

And sure enough, that's exactly what happened. The station

changed formats and Simon was out of a job. His chances of getting back on the air are not great, but that doesn't diminish what he did during his on-air career.

Simon's credibility was based solely on his untrained ability to analyze sports situations and comment knowledgeably. In a sense, he was the true representative of the sports fans in his audience. It is a prime example of an ability many people have, but few recognize as a marketable asset.

Key #2: The Importance of Desire

Passion for the work may be the most important key to developing expertise. Let's take a truly absurd example. If you grew up on an Indian reservation in northeast Arizona but wanted to become a trusted authority on Irish dancing, you could do it. If you want anything enough, it is possible if you have the desire.

The problem with desire is that there may be only a finite amount in each of us. For instance, if you want to become a great Irish dancer, you may have to devote your entire energy to it. The biggest roadblock to success for most people is selecting among many possible choices. You have only so much energy. There are only so many hours in a day. If you spend those hours dancing, you may not have time for much else.

An effective gauge of desire is to ask what you would give up to accomplish your goal. Would you stop watching television in the evening to practice? Would you turn down a vacation to compete in your specialty? Is your specialty important enough for you to give up precious time with your family and friends?

A burning desire is one of the most important keys to making assets marketable.

Key #3: Getting There First

Those with an extreme desire to accomplish something often get there first. Being one of the first to attempt to become a trusted authority in a particular area has tremendous advantages — and a few drawbacks.

Because you are first, you may get credit for a new and different idea. You are, by definition, unique. In your dealings with the media, uniqueness is good only to a certain extent. It is true that when one member of the media gets interested in a story, the rest of the media want it. This is the herd mentality often attributed to the press. But ideas that might be considered too new can confuse the media. Newness is often suspect, and so you must take the time to educate the media about your area of expertise.

There is risk involved in introducing new concepts to the public. Your ideas might not be embraced or you may not be taken seriously. If the development of a product demands an investment of money and time, you risk losing money and wasting time.

The naming of products is a good example of the risks all of us take. Authors tell us that when they first name a book, the title often doesn't sound right. It sounds like something made up, which it is. How could anything made up like that possibly be real? But something or someone creates everything. Only over time does a title or product name begin to sound like something real. When people begin to call and ask for the book by name, it gains a life of its own.

The patience to educate people is essential. You must tell the media and public why your area of expertise is important, what it will do for them and what they can expect from it in the future.

You must be brave in the face of indifference or outright scorn by the media and public that are unfamiliar with your area of expertise.

FIVE KEYS TO DEVELOPING EXPERTISE

By educating people about your passion, you are blazing a trail for authoritative people to come.

You establish yourself as an expert in the field by getting there first.

Key #4: Researching the Product

Research is essential to the development of an effective product that is imbued with Credibility Power. So what do we mean by "product" in this context? To the 19th century mind, products were mass-produced on factory floors. For the first three quarters of the 20th century, products were mostly thought of as items in slick packages on store shelves. Gradually products came to mean anything that could be sold, including intangibles such as insurance policies or types of mortgages and information obtainable in a seminar or on an infomercial.

Seminar organizations consider what they do as producing and delivering product, whether it is instruction about how to set up a living trust, raise more resourceful children or buy real estate without investing your own money. Products are what infomercials are selling in all forms.

Research can confirm the uniqueness of a product and let you determine how the power of credibility can help you sell this product.

Key #5: Focusing Your Efforts

For most people, becoming a trusted authority in one specific field takes all of your time and energy. Martha Stewart is not an expert in home remodeling or home sales. She is the queen of home décor.

Michael Bohdan is not a big-game hunter or a breeder of champion dogs. The creatures he knows best are little household pests.

A moving target of expertise is confusing to both the media and the public. You should always focus your attention on a subject area that is manageable and can be learned.

Case History:
His Job Is Finding Your Job

Martin Birnbach had a wide range of expertise in business, including sales and marketing, when he set out to become a trusted authority. But he didn't attempt to become an authority in such a broad category. He began a career-counseling business and decided to become his city's leading expert in jobs and careers.

He became president of the local association that represents the employment industry and then earned a spot on the national board. These posts put him in a position to do occasional pieces on local television.

Opportunities surfaced after that preparation. There was a regular radio show on employment, a newspaper column, a spot on local television news and a cable TV show. In each of these ventures, Birnbach could have branched out into general discussions of the business climate or economic conditions. But he focused all of his media efforts on jobs and careers.

He produced a videotape titled *Winning the Job You Really Want* and a series of audiotapes called *The Job Quest.*

"We have found that as long as we stay focused, one thing feeds another," Birnbach says. "Whatever opportunities we have, they must relate to jobs and careers."

When the number of job applicants exceeds the positions avail-

FIVE KEYS TO DEVELOPING EXPERTISE

able, he offers seminars that attract thousands of people wanting to know how to get a job. When there are more jobs than applicants, he works with corporations on how to attract the best workers.

Even the compensation Birnbach receives for much of his work is tightly focused. For his radio show, part of his compensation comes in the form of advertising for his career-counseling business.

"You see, everything I do is tied to jobs and careers," he notes. "I don't do anything outside of that."

In your quest to become a trusted authority, you must maintain a tight focus on one specific area of expertise.

CREDIBILITY POWER

PART TWO

How to Set Credibility Power into Motion

CHAPTER 6

IN THIS CHAPTER
- Begin With Organization
- Select the Correct Media
- Know Your Limitations
- Set Goals
- Plow Right In

Getting Started

Like almost everything else in life, the first steps to beginning a venture into Credibility Power are the most important.

GETTING STARTED

> **CREDIBILITY PROFILE**
>
> Benjamin Dover made his way from busted dealmaker to the guru of credit counseling to conservative commentator. His personal experience with bill collectors helped him reach a position of trusted authority.

Few people have begun their quest to CP respectability from a worse position than Benjamin Dover has. Dover was a freewheeling dealmaker in the early 1980s. "I did promotional deals," he says. "I worked with rock-and-roll people. I did some sports-oriented promotional deals. I dabbled in real estate and oil and gas."

It was a time when money flowed fast and loose, and most people thought it would flow on forever. In 1986, though, the economy faltered. The money spigot went dry. And Dover found himself unable to raise capital for his various investments.

"Because of poor business decisions, I was late on every bill I owed," he says. "That's when I felt the wrath of the debt collectors firsthand.

Dover was working himself out of his financial jam in 1989 when he was almost killed in a motorcycle accident. "I woke up on the pavement with a whole new attitude," he recalls. "After 12 surgeries and $200,000 in medical bills, I had a different view of the world."

For three years, he struggled to recuperate from the accident with three-hour physical therapy sessions three times a week. In the therapist's office, he spoke with a man about the drudgery of the recovery process and its inevitable result — the indignity of dealing with bill collectors.

The man suggested to Dover that they team up to publish a book on the subject. The result was *STOP IT!*, a book on dealing with debts and the harassment of bill collectors. This was followed by *Life After Debt: The Blueprint for Surviving In America's Credit Society*. This second book topped out at No. 8 on the national bestseller list and became required reading in one university business course. His next book, *Back Off! The Definitive Guide to Stopping Collection Agency Harassment*, sold out its first printing in less than two hours, thanks to an appearance by Dover on *The Oprah Winfrey Show*.

Dover is a popular television guest on national and regional shows and his advice column runs in several major newspapers. He does a syndicated radio show and is on the lecture circuit. Dover employs most of the media available to those who use the power of credibility. His position as an authority on consumer credit grows by the day.

"Writing a book was the cornerstone of my credibility campaign," he notes. "The first book was fairly simple to write because it focused on a very narrow segment of the business society. It focused on something that was a real hot button."

He believes that anybody can publish a book. "We self-published," he explains. "My motivation for self-publishing was not because I couldn't get a major publisher to do the book. It was quite the opposite. I self-published because I knew the amount of money publishers make."

Dover was intent on making that money himself, and he has. This quest has kept him moving, promoting his expertise. He finds the promotion gratifying because he feels he is doing good things for others while he increases his own marketability.

"This is the most gratifying thing I've done in my life because I know that I'm changing people's lives every day," he says. "I have an impact on people every time they pick up one of my books, hear me on the radio or see me on television."

Dover has not only maintained his media position over the years. He has, in fact, widened his scope. Where once he was identified only as an expert in consumer credit, his syndicated radio program has expanded his role as a conservative commentator on a number of public affairs questions.

The source of his motivation is that lowly starting point in the mid-1980s. "I know how bad I felt and how I got my brains beaten out back then," he says. "I didn't think there was any hope. I wish there had been someone like me back then. There were times when I didn't want to go on."

Begin with Organization

This book is built around examples of people using the power of credibility successfully, so you can start to organize your thoughts and actions around those successful models.

A natural chain of events begins the process. First comes the book or an article, then the radio show, then television or an infomercial.

Then comes a successful series of seminars. Not everyone does it this way or in this order, but the most successful CP practitioners follow a systematic process of leveraging one medium into another.

In later chapters, we will discuss how each of these successful practitioners creates or manipulates media. You will learn specifically how anyone can make these media opportunities happen. But for now, you will want to concentrate on organizing the overall strategy of the venture into Credibility Power.

Select the Correct Media

Selection of the media you want to employ in your venture involves individual choices driven by several considerations:

Trustworthiness or Credibility of the Media Form — Various media have a built-in trust factor that people assign to them. Books carry an enormous reservoir of trustworthiness. This is a quality we know about books even before we examine the actual contents of the book. It's why many of the personalities we profiled say that a writing a book — more than any other use of Credibility Power — made them authorities in their field.

In past years, there was a perceived difference in credibility between books brought to the marketplace by a conventional publisher and those that were self-published. In some circles, there is still more cachet to works published under the Simon & Schuster banner, for instance, than Uncle Harry's Press. But that game means more to publishing insiders.

If you follow some of the rules for presenting and packaging books that we outline in a later chapter, the average person will see lit-

GETTING STARTED

tle difference between a book from a major New York publisher and one you warehoused in your garage. In fact, most people fail to notice who published most of the books they purchase.

At the other end of the credibility spectrum, paid advertising is not considered as trustworthy and the claims made in paid advertising may be suspect. Most other media have moderate to high credibility.

Control of the Message — Controlling the message is an important part of establishing Credibility Power. If you are to become a trusted authority in an area, the message must be YOURS.

Media differ by the amount of control the CP practitioner has over the message being sent out to the public. When you prepare and present a seminar, you control everything that is said except for the responses of seminar participants. The same goes for video and audiotapes and newsletters prepared for sale or free distribution.

Examples of media that offer little message control are stories disseminated to newspapers and magazines through the media relations process. You may distribute the exact story you want to the news media, but there is no guarantee that after the writing and editing process it will even remotely resemble your original work. In a later chapter, you will learn how to minimize that problem, which is an inherent part of media and public relations.

Control can differ even within types of media. A self-published book remains well within your control from the original manuscript to the finished product. Say you hire people to help you write, design or distribute a book. The people working for you should give suggestions but remain ultimately under your control. If you are fortunate enough to sell your book to a publisher, control of the message is negotiable with the publisher taking the financial risk.

CREDIBILITY POWER

Risk for the CP Practitioner — Measure your risk of using selected media in time and dollars. If you appear for free on a local television program, you have a very small investment of time or money. Any book that you write and publish involves a substantial investment in time at the word processor.

The original draft of this book, for instance, took an average of four hours a day, five days a week for three months. But we spent as many hours doing interviews before the writing could begin. And we invested more hours editing and rewriting following the original draft.

Self-publishing a book also means that you, the CP practitioner, pay for everything. Expenses for a book the size and quality of this one, including registration with the proper agencies and printing 5,000 copies, would be from $11,000 to $16,000.

If a publishing house accepts a book, the house pays all of the expenses. That's why publishers retain a larger proportion of the profits on the sale of the book.

Ease of Entry into a Medium — Under the most common con-

For this book, expenses included the following:

Securing International Standard Book Number	$ 125
Securing bar code	$ 30
Registration with Library of Congress	$ 25
Freelance editing services	$ 1,500
Book design and layout	$ 2,500
Printing of 5,000 copies	$ 7,500
TOTAL	$11,680

GETTING STARTED

ditions, how likely are you to be successful using these media? For the most part, anyone can self-publish a book, while finding a publisher for your work may be more difficult.

You may not be successful getting radio or television stations to hire you to host a show on your area of expertise, and it might be difficult to convince a newspaper or magazine to run your work. It may be easier to convince broadcast stations to use you as a one-time guest or newspapers and magazines to write about you.

Creating seminars and tapes may be relatively easy, while convincing members of the public to attend your seminar or purchase your tapes can be difficult.

Penetration of Your Message — An important measure of media effectiveness is the sheer number of people your message can reach. If market penetration were the only measure of CP effectiveness, television would be the medium to emphasize. There are more television sets in America than there are homes. Television actors and news people are better known and recognized than famous writers. That's the nature of a visual medium.

One author found out about the power of television while promoting a regional book. He had made several personal appearances and the book was selling, but the publisher didn't have it in all stores statewide. Then one morning he appeared on the top-rated local "coffee talk" show in the market. The five-minute segment began at 9:50 a.m. The publisher reported that within 25 minutes of his appearance, local bookstore employees began calling. They didn't have the book, and their customers wanted to buy copies. With television, the effect is immediate and often huge. The same can be said for radio, although radio audiences are increasingly fragmented. Books tend to reach a smaller audience, while seminars and tapes often reach even less.

Commitment and Demands on the Receiver of the Message — It's important to gauge the demands you are making on your audience, in terms of time and money. Which is easier for the audience, reading a book or watching a five-minute television segment? Which involves more of a money commitment, paying for an all-day seminar or the morning paper?

The amount of commitment you are asking from your audience often will determine how receptive that audience is to your message and, therefore, how many people you will reach.

Durability of Message — While broadcasting reaches the greatest number of people, no message is more durable than that in books. Books continue to work for years to come. The effectiveness of a message in a book continues until your message is outdated or you publish another book.

The written word has always been more durable than what is said on radio or television. The fact that you can easily revisit the thoughts on paper adds to the durability.

The chart on the next page examines each of the media strategies that are part of credibility marketing in terms of the seven media considerations already outlined.

Know Your Limitations

Lack of money, time, energy or expertise can dilute the power of credibility, but only if you allow it. Without the proper financial backing, self-publishing a book is not a good option. The same goes for producing an infomercial or a series of video or audiotapes.

A glance at our table of media considerations offers direction.

GETTING STARTED

Media Strategies	MEDIA CONSIDERATIONS						
	Trust/ Credibility	Control of Message	Risk (Time and Money)	Ability to Accomplish	Penetration of Message	Demand on Receiver of Message (Time and Money)	Durability of Message
Books							
Self-Published	High	High	High (Time, $)	High	Moderate	High	High
Conventional Publishing	High	Low	High (Time)	Low	Moderate	High	High
Seminars	Moderate	High	Moderate	Moderate	Low	High	Low
Media Star (Radio or TV host, newspaper or magazine writer)	Moderate	Moderate	Low	Low	High	Low	Low
Media Guest (Radio or TV guest, contribute story ideas to newspapers or magazines)	High	Low	Low	Low	High	Low	Low
Audio and Videotapes	Moderate	High	High ($)	Moderate	Low	Moderate	High
Newsletters	Moderate	High	Moderate	Moderate	Moderate	Low	Moderate
Infomercials	Low	High	High ($)	High	High	Low	Low
Internet	Low	High	Low	High	Moderate	Low	Low
Advertising	Paid ads are not included as part of developing authority. They inform people, but there is little trust or respect accorded them. They can be helpful at the cashing-in phase.						

High = Much or very, such as very easy to accomplish.
Low = Little or not much, such as little demand on the receiver of the message.
Moderate = Some or somewhat, such as a message being somewhat durable.

Working to become a regular on radio or television or a regular contributor to newspapers or magazines on your area of expertise involves a smaller commitment of money and time. A media relations campaign to get an occasional spot on the broadcast media or convince print publications to write stories on a given area usually involves even a smaller amount of time and almost no money.

Lack of money often brings out the natural creativity in those who use Credibility Power. Remember fitness expert Larry North's campaign to become better known as the arbiter of a healthy lifestyle? The fact that he spent the time to learn the public relations business, rather than just hiring a PR representative, expanded his own abilities and made him a better marketer. Even after he published his first book, North continued to devise ways of becoming better known. That's when he went to restaurant managers and suggested a healthy menu item. Everywhere he went, there was a Larry North plate and the resulting publicity.

> You can never have too much information when trying to become a trusted authority on a subject.

Creative solutions can compensate for personality limitations. The only sure stopper among your limitations would be a shortage of expertise. That is a problem that must be cured for you to be successful. Expertise generates Credibility Power, and expertise that you purchase from outside vendors can only carry you so far. Without expertise, you are not even on your way to a position of trusted authority. This is one of the major differences between credibility marketing and paid advertising. Because paid ads involve mostly image making, you can actually promote yourself through this method without knowing very much

GETTING STARTED

about the subject area. A credibility campaign is more about the details.

Someone interviewing you for local television wants to inform and entertain viewers. This requires information, and all reporters value the extended remarks offered by the best interviewees.

Notice the reaction of local news reporters after asking a question of an eyewitness to an accident. The person answers the question, but often the reporter leaves the microphone in the person's face. Clearly, the reporter wants more information, but the person who witnessed the accident has told everything he or she knows. Sometimes, the person will feel compelled to launch into more talk on unfamiliar subjects, and the lack of expertise will be evident to the viewing public. That is the point at which the expert, as opposed to the lay person, ingratiates himself or herself to the media by offering extended remarks on a central subject.

Always approach media opportunities loaded with an overabundance of factual information. There is no such thing as having too much information. If you don't have all the facts you need, go out and gather them.

Set Goals

Armed with all the information needed to generate Credibility Power, you should set realistic goals for your program. Construct a timetable with realistic timeframes. Is it realistic to assume that in the next 90 days, you can accomplish the following: become an expert in your field, write and publish a book, appear on national television and conduct a series of seminars complete with back-of-the-room sales of video and audiotapes?

Even if you could forego sleep for the next three months, it's unlikely that you could convince everyone else needed to accomplish such a feat to concentrate only on your projects.

It is best to set goals within the time limits you have. Assume that it would take six months to write a book and another six months either to find a publisher or decide to self-publish. During that year, you might also prepare material for a series of seminars based on the ideas found in the book. That material would correspond with the text of the book and could generate ideas for stories that might be sent to the local media.

To become a regular guest on a local radio or television show, be prepared to face rejection at first. Sometimes you must become known to the program's host by offering ideas that could prove helpful to the show's ratings. Ratings are important, and ideas that will help keep ratings high are considered valuable.

Goal setting can require leveraging assets for maximum effect.

Gaining your first foothold in the media is the most difficult. Below are some logical steps to realizing your media goals.

- Convince a local newspaper editor or reporter to run a story about your area of expertise and quote you as an expert.
- Armed with the actual tear sheet of that article, convince local groups to invite you to speak on the subject to their members. After all, the newspaper has deemed you the local expert. Be sure to keep copies of the group's program, with your name prominently displayed, along with copies of any newspaper ads or transcripts of radio or television advertising announcing the talk.
- With proof of your expert status, you should be able to talk your way onto a local radio or television show.

GETTING STARTED

Pretty soon, you can have a scrapbook of media successes as a résumé of your ability to communicate your expertise. You may also have a much greater understanding of the best way to communicate in your subject area, an important factor in this process.

Plow Right In

You don't have to ask anyone's permission to begin harnessing Credibility Power. You might begin with the following:

- List the major themes you want to communicate to the public about your area of expertise.
- Write down what the media would find interesting about that expertise.
- List the media you would like to explore and any possible contacts you might have at media outlets. Maybe you attend church with a news reporter or your nephew walks the treadmill at his fitness center alongside the city's top news anchor. Chance encounters can be the most productive.
- Draft letters to the various editors or news directors you want to approach. A later chapter will deal with specific ways to make those approaches. These letters simply put your ideas on paper, where you can examine them.
- Write a sample press release on your subject area.
- Compile a list of your Credibility Power assets. Examples might be the ability to write or speak in public.
- Also compile a list of your CP deficits, so that you can determine where you might need outside help. (See "Seeking Outside Assistance," Chapter 10.) In fact, you may want to hire a PR consultant to help you with this list.

CREDIBILITY POWER

At this early stage, it is essential for you to write down everything and note everybody you know who can help. Don't edit any of these thoughts. You can cull your prospects later.

CHAPTER 7

IN THIS CHAPTER
- Create a Unique Persona
- Understand the Media
- Take Risks

Creating the Winning Product: Yourself

Many of us tend to be our own worst enemy. To successfully generate Credibility Power, often we must shape and mold ourselves into our most valuable product.

CREATING THE WINNING PRODUCT: YOURSELF

> **CREDIBILITY PROFILE**
>
> If anyone ever invented himself, it is Zig Ziglar. The cookware salesman turned world-famous motivational speaker and best-selling author, now in his 70s, travels the world delivering his message of positive thought.

Zig Ziglar is unique among credibility marketers. Most people attempting to maintain a position of trusted authority struggle to find what is new, improved and different to separate themselves from others in their field.

In most cases, we encourage this struggle. But Ziglar has been remarkably consistent over his career. He delivers much the same message he did three decades ago. Branded "America's Merchant of Hope" in a recent magazine article, Ziglar still uses many of the sayings he originated — or borrowed from other master motivators — to construct his positivist philosophy beginning in the 1950s.

Examples: "If this doesn't light your fire, your wood is wet," and a quote he borrowed: "You don't have to be great to start, but you have to start to be great." These and other sayings pepper the speeches he makes before an ever-widening audience. These appearances earn him up to $50,000 each and he makes about 50 each year to sales and corporate groups. He shares his thoughts in the Zig Ziglar Performance Planner and the 10 million audiotapes he has sold at his seminars. And the same words of wisdom have made their way into his 17 books, which have cumulatively sold more than 5 million copies.

Although the field of motivation and self-help has become more sophisticated, segmented and, some would say, "slick" in 30 years, Ziglar himself is the same as he was back when he started — only more so.

In fact, the secret to his success may be that he has never found the need to reinvent himself. He follows much the same routine each day. He is unfailingly kind and polite to people, as well as completely positive about their prospects.

He tells them "You were designed for accomplishment, engineered for success and endowed with the seeds of greatness." He tells himself that today he will break 70 on the golf course, even though he has never shot 70 in his life. He reads the local newspaper, various inspirational magazines and books and the Bible. He avoids negative stories in favor of the inspiring and blessed. And he still prepares for three to five hours before each talk to make certain he will be at his best.

He never tires of the routine, never rebels against being Zig Ziglar. It has created a positive-thinking empire worth millions for him. And, by all accounts, his message of motivation and success has created plenty of worldly goods for those who pay to hear, see and read him.

Hilary Hinton Ziglar, nicknamed "Zig" in his boyhood, intended to open a butcher shop in his hometown of Yazoo City, Mississippi. But the closest he came to the food business was a job selling stainless steel cookware door to door. Jobs were hard to come by just after his release from the U.S. Navy following World War II. Ziglar had nothing to his name but a reputation for good character and a positive atti-

CREATING THE WINNING PRODUCT: YOURSELF

tude. He would give himself pep talks about how things would improve and his cookware sales would increase. And as they increased, he was promoted to supervisor.

In 1952, he attended a motivational speech and saw how his life could be changed forever. Ziglar continued with the cookware company as a sales trainer, but his future was made as a speaker to civic groups, churches and schools.

He became an instructor at the Dale Carnegie Institute in New York City in 1955. He became a full-time public speaker in 1970 and soon was one of the most sought-after motivational talkers in the country.

"For 20 years, I was scratchin' for speeches to give," Ziglar recalls. "But I haven't solicited an engagement since 1972."

He has been featured in *The New York Times, The Washington Post, Fortune, Esquire, Success* and *Time*. His national television appearances include *Today, Hour of Power, 20/20* and *60 Minutes*.

Fellow motivational trainer Peter Lowe of the Peter Lowe Success Seminars says of Ziglar: "Of all the great people who speak at our seminars, from Christopher Reeve to Norman Schwarzkopf to Colin Powell, Zig still gets the best response. He knows how to reach people in a way that no one else can."

Even though he has given essentially the same speech 500 times, Ziglar rewrites his notes and adds new quips, jokes and human interest stories to make certain the next speech will be crisp and fresh. "I make every talk like it's going to be my last," he explains, "because one day I will make my last talk, and I have no way of knowing when that will be. So I give it my best shot every time."

Ziglar self-published his first book, *See You at the Top*. It is now in its 58th printing and has sold more than 1.6 million copies. He has written two books on selling, *Secrets of Closing the Sale* and *Ziglar on*

Selling. He has also written books on family and spiritual topics, such as *Raising Positive Kids in a Negative World, Dear Family, Confessions of a Happy Christian* and *Confessions of a Grieving Christian*.

Besides the books he's written, Ziglar's practical philosophy has been incorporated into an extensive array of audio, video and printed training tools in addition to seminars and workshops. *ZigOnline*, an Internet-based, on-demand audio training system that offers "instant access to the same success secrets that have helped millions worldwide," is available on the World Wide Web at www.zigbiz.net.

Ziglar's works have been translated into 35 languages and dialects, and he has received several thousand letters from all over the world saying that his materials have enriched peoples' lives. Companies of all sizes, as well as individuals, prisons and churches use these materials.

Even at an advanced age and with all of his experience, Ziglar still reads several hours each day for new ideas, examples, jokes, analogies and illustrations. But with his success over these many years, he sees no reason to change his forward-looking, faith-based philosophy.

Create a Unique Persona

The public and the media are always looking for new, fresh personalities with something different to say. Remember what Bruce Jenner said about his television opportunities? He knew that he had a limited amount of time to interest the public while he was learning the television business. In four years, another world's greatest athlete would come into the limelight and push him out of it if he was not fully established. This is a prime example of prudent advanced planning that enhances your Credibility Power.

CREATING THE WINNING PRODUCT: YOURSELF

The best planning by those who aren't celebrities or world-class athletes is to create a unique persona that will help carry your message to the public and the media.

Persona is an individual's outer personality presented to others. A persona is not something fake or dishonest. It must be interesting and the person who creates it must be comfortable with it.

Michael Bohdan created the persona of a pest-control man with a sense of humor. That's also the way Bohdan really is. He is a pest controller who can laugh at himself. His humor and honesty sell the persona for him.

Dr. Phil McGraw's persona of Dr. "Tell It Like It Is" Phil reflects his straight-talking, forthright nature. It is just slightly exaggerated for more dynamic effect in the mass media.

So how do you create a persona? Let's see how Zig Ziglar did it. First, he isolated what he does best, which is to inspire people with a positive message.

Second, Ziglar has presented virtually the same image over the years. This makes him seem like a throwback to another era. But it's comforting to people who value traditional ways of doing things.

Third, he has remained true to his ideals and continues to work hard before every talk to get his speech just right. This steadfastness is authentic Ziglar, and it also contributes to his unique persona. The lesson he teaches is clear: Find something that works, stick with it, improve it and continue to make it yours.

Case History: His Company with the Little Red Trucks

If you fix appliances for a living, how do you create an effective persona for use in local promotional efforts? Ask Ahron Katz, chairman and founder of a local appliance and air conditioning company.

Katz started his business in 1976. He knew that appliance repair and replacement had little sex appeal in the public's mind. Still, he wanted to establish a distinctive difference between his company and other similar organizations. "I've always been very interested in marketing," Katz says. "So I bought six red trucks and put our 'A' logo on them."

For years, Katz marketed the logo on billboards and in other forms of advertising. Then in the early '90s, he took his story to radio.

There are two different ways to generate Credibility Power on radio. The traditional route is for radio station management to build a news segment or a show around you and your expertise, as in the case of Leon Simon. The credibility factor is very high in this instance, since someone other than you is proclaiming you the expert. The challenge is to get station management to recognize your superiority. If you don't know someone at the station or become known in your community for some other Credibility Power ventures, how do they know about you and why should you get such an opportunity?

The second scenario gives you a little push in the direction of Credibility Power recognition. With so many radio stations in markets of all sizes, many news and talk stations simply sell time to people who have something to market. Depending on market size and the station's ratings, a Saturday afternoon show can cost from $800 to $3,000 per hour. Many weekend shows feature fitness experts, financial planners and other professionals who are so well-paid for their services that they can afford to invest this kind of money to build credibility and their businesses.

Katz made it to the airwaves under both scenarios. He was asked to be a guest on an established radio show after signing a contract to advertise his business. After handling two guest segments well, Katz was asked to host the show. Advertising on the station helped him come to the attention of station managers, who were intrigued by his radio presence. Katz hosted this show for 18 months, then decided to leave radio for awhile and concentrate on converting the opportunities this exposure gave him into business growth.

Only when he discontinued his hosting duties did he see how vital the exposure was. So he contracted with another station for 90 minutes of airtime each Saturday afternoon. On his program, *Ask Ahron*, Katz fields questions about repairing and replacing appliances. Since he controls the content, he can bring guests on the program and sell advertising spots that help defray his costs. To the listening public, there is little difference in credibility between this and shows that are produced by the station.

But does this kind of paid program gain marketing results that make it worthwhile? "I wasn't sure at first," Katz says. "It was really eight or nine months before I realized what a boon it is to my business."

The show made him a minor local celebrity and has brought greater name identification to his company. "I began to identify my company on the air as the one with the little red trucks, and that has stuck," he says. "Some of our trucks aren't so little anymore, and we have 70 of them."

Katz' impressive promotional abilities have established him as a leader in his field. He was the subject of a May 1997 editorial in *Success* magazine, which called him a "sales visionary." An article in the November 1996 issue of *Appliance Service News* described him as a "superstar" in his industry. He writes occasional columns for *Contracting Business* magazine and is a popular after-dinner speaker.

The company reached such a prominent position that Katz sold it to a national firm in 1997. He stayed on to run the business, but now he has ideas about generating more Credibility Power. He has talked to management at the radio station that carries his program about having him substitute for one of the station's conservative commentators during vacation season. He takes every opportunity to speak in public, participate in charity affairs and project his persona outside the world of appliances.

For Ahron Katz, being identified as the fix-it man is not enough. He is intent on extending his reach to the world at large.

Case History: Enhance the Trust Factor

Carol Miller was a financial planner who wanted to branch out into other endeavors that would be exciting and profitable. It was early in the 1990s, and she thought about the meaning of the phrase identifying that 10-year period — the decade of information.

"A friend of mine and I just sat down and brainstormed about it," Miller recalls, "and we came up with the idea of finding information on travel and relocating in various areas of the world, and where people can find employment in these places."

Neither Miller nor her friend had any experience in travel, employment, writing, editing or publishing. There was no reason for anyone to trust their work in these areas. They simply had an idea, and they hired a researcher to gather the information for them.

"We sent letters to all the major world-class vacation spots asking if they would like to be in a book listing jobs at resorts," Miller explains.

So how did she know people would buy such a book or have any interest in it? "If you've got a product and you use the marketing techniques that are available, you can generally find the target market for it," she maintains.

Miller was deluged with information, and from that she fashioned a book that she self-published and distributed through direct mail.

"It crossed my mind to have it in bookstores," she says. "But I'm a marketing person. I'd rather be responsible for that function than having to wait for people to come in and buy something."

She placed small ads for the book in newspapers around the country. She hired telemarketers and installed 800 numbers. The first month she received 1,500 calls and sold at least 750 books at the cover price of $49.95.

> **This project seemed less like selling books and more like marketing a product.**

The book was off and running and Miller continued to sell books until she sold the entire operation — at a hefty profit — some months later. Miller proved she could begin with a good idea and, armed with her own marketing ability and expertise that she purchased, bring it to life.

Understand the Market

A crucial aspect of Credibility Power is identifying your target audience and understanding what motivates that particular group.

As a credibility marketer, you cannot afford to market to everyone. Trying to appeal to the tastes of everyone would be an unrealistic undertaking that's too expensive and time consuming.

CREDIBILITY POWER

Focus your efforts on a specific market and go after your customers with a vengeance. Remember that even someone as famous as Martha Stewart focuses her efforts. Her market does not include everyone. She appeals only to those people who want to present a more elegant home life. Fitness expert Larry North focuses his efforts on people who want to live a healthier life. Attorney Ike Vanden Eykel is interested in people who are seeking to divorce in a more civilized manner.

Case History:
Getting What You're Worth

Bill Bishop focuses his efforts on training salespeople from many different industries. He knows salespeople well, since he spent the early part of his career selling television advertising and cable TV subscriptions. Bishop enjoyed success in sales at an early age. As a beginning door-to-door salesman, he signed up more people the first week than his four experienced co-workers combined.

This success translated into healthy earnings and made him want to sell more. "I knew selling was the career for me if I wanted to get paid what I was worth and not just take home a salary, which is what someone else thinks I'm worth," Bishop says.

His training consisted of only a two-day course taught by his sales manager. But as he sold more and more, he could see how additional training might enhance his abilities.

A customer saw that he had potential as a salesman and suggested the teachings of Jay Douglas Edwards, known by many as the father of sales training and a man who led motivational seminars long before Zig Ziglar, Tom Hopkins and others popularized the notion. Edwards recorded his work before the invention of cassette tapes, so the customer loaned Bishop three 33-rpm records of Edwards' sales-training seminars.

Bishop took a Dale Carnegie course and then went to the library and began to check out books on selling. "Over the next several years, I read 76 books on selling," Bishop says. "I outlined each chapter until I had hundreds of pages on how to sell."

Bishop reached expert status incrementally, starting with an in-house sales course, adding the teachings of Edwards and Carnegie and all those other books on salesmanship. This gradual increase in sales knowledge helped him understand the art of selling and inspired him to think about producing his own training products. The knowledge and expertise helped him when he made the decision to write his own book on salesmanship.

"I wrote and self-published this book and started selling it by mail order and, presto chango, that made me a sales trainer," Bishop says. "Most of the people who read the book were individual salespeople, but some were the owners of companies or the managers of sales organizations. They were impressed with my approach. They would call me and ask if I did seminars. I had never done one before, but I told them I could."

Bishop believes the best salespeople are open to information that will help them become better. Helping them toward that goal made him the expert.

"I could try to beat people into saying I'm a sales trainer," Bishop says. "A few people might go along with it, but most would resist. But once I wrote the book, they said that I must be an expert trainer, since I wrote the book. Being an author gives you credibility. I have since written many articles for magazines that salespeople read, and that gives me a tremendous amount of credibility."

CREDIBILITY POWER

Bishop believes many salespeople feel victimized by trainers who entice them into continued purchases in order to obtain worthwhile information.

"I don't like it when I pay money to go to someone's seminar, and they tell me I will learn A, B and C. I find that I can learn 'A' and 'B.' But to learn 'C' I have to spend even more money to buy the tapes or the book or come to the next seminar. I feel cheated and defrauded. So when someone takes my seminar, I give them the whole course, everything I know."

Bishop followed his first book with a sequel. He intended to publish a third book, but found that his audience wanted something else.

"I kept getting letters from readers who loved the book, thought it was great" Bishop says. "They said to contact them if I ever put it on a cassette tape. Salespeople want instant gratification. A set of tapes has a higher perceived value than a book. I can sell a set of audiotapes for considerably more than a book."

> If a book sells, tapes and software might also. Listen to your prospective customers about the value of particular products.

His understanding of market needs has spurred development of a variety of products. He recorded a set of tapes on how to sell. He followed that with a set of tapes on how to prospect. Then he added a set on how to prospect specifically for the life insurance industry. Next came a software tool to help his customers implement his training. He released a set of 18 monthly motivational posters, and moved on to video products.

"A video program is very good for small group training," Bishop says. "Five, 10, 20 salespeople can watch a video. So I'm trying to expand my market and expand my credibility by covering more markets."

Case History: Rolling the Dice on a Media Career

Any display of Credibility Power involves some element of entrepreneurship, which requires risk-taking. That's what Clyde Goldberg told his wife when he established his investment and retirement strategies firm several years ago.

For 25 years before that, Goldberg had been a top sales executive for large insurance companies in California, Texas and finally Syracuse, New York. He was back in Syracuse working for one of these companies when he vowed to form his own firm. When he decided to make that great leap, he wanted his wife to know everything would be OK.

"The first thing we did was figure out our living expenses for a year," Goldberg says, "and I wrote my wife a check for that amount. I wanted her to feel secure."

Goldberg also took risks with his marketing budget. To grow the name recognition and credibility he felt were important in marketing his products and services, he ran ads on radio and television stations in the Syracuse market. The ads began to attract business, so he committed to hosting a Sunday call-in show called *DollarWise* on a local radio station. This show was paid programming — Goldberg paid the station for the time and used that time as he saw fit. With increasing media experience, he became a featured guest on a television show about financial issues as well as an expert commentator for another

CREDIBILITY POWER

local station doing morning and evening news segments. He leveraged those opportunities into a newspaper column on financial strategies and was asked to teach adult education classes on financial planning, retirement and investments.

The subject of all these activities is the same as his motto: "Life is tough — retirement doesn't have to be."

Goldberg uses media exposure to promote an ongoing series of public financial seminars he conducts all across Central New York. Much of his business comes from these seminars.

"There is an implied credibility to seeing me on television or in a newspaper column," Goldberg says. "These credibility marketing efforts all have my picture on them, not because I'm so good looking, but because people are more comfortable responding when they see who's behind the ad. People like to do business with someone they know. When we meet they feel as if they already know me. It's never a first meeting."

Investment counselor Clyde Goldberg uses radio and other media to get across his marketing point, that "life is tough—retirement doesn't have to be."

The risk for someone who can organize a venture in Credibility Power as well as Goldberg can is that you might concentrate your efforts on becoming a full-time media star and neglect your business. Goldberg feels you must understand when you hit the point of diminishing returns. He purchased the time for his radio show and resold it to an attorney, an accountant, a long-term care specialist and an investment advisor who paid for much of the airtime. He also sold ads on the program as well as running those for his business. He was getting great exposure and covering most of his costs. CP practitioners who concentrate on selling their airtime can actually make money from this venture.

As effective as the radio show was for him, Goldberg discontinued it to concentrate on his core business. He may host a radio program again when he believes the time is right, but he would like to try a different format.

"There is no real risk for someone like me who hates cold-calling," Goldberg says. "Gaining credibility from the media saves you from having to make those calls. All insurance salespeople hate cold calls. They drive people out of this business. I believe I've found a better way."

CHAPTER 8

IN THIS CHAPTER
- Traditional Book Publishing
- The New Book Business
- Self-Publishing
- Newsletter Concept
- Newsletter Production
- Media Relations

CP's Top Tool: The Written Word

The quickest route from expert to authority is through written communications. Look at the ways writing can enhance credibility.

> ## CREDIBILITY PROFILE
>
> Ken Fisher, columnist for *Forbes* magazine and a prolific author, was a "money man" with no demonstrated writing ability when he set out to separate himself from others in his field.

Writing was the last skill Ken Fisher thought he would master when he decided to produce a book called *Super Stocks* in the mid-1980s. Fisher hated English class in high school and college. He had no experience writing anything more ambitious than a buy or sell order. The young money manager did not see his book as a literary venture. He approached it as an opportunity to showcase his investment expertise.

With that in mind, Fisher gathered a mountain of factual information and hired talent where he felt he was lacking. A local business journalist helped him edit the book. He read as much as he could about book promotion and found that publishers get enthusiastic when famous people endorse the work.

At a business forum, he had what he calls a "light interaction" with Jim Michaels, then the editor of *Forbes*. Fisher sent the editor several pages of his manuscript. Michaels liked what he read and contributed a quote for the dust jacket of the book. He also published some of Fisher's work in the magazine.

The budding financial guru was on his way to having his book launched by the publishing arm of the Dow Jones Company, and his articles were being published in one of the nation's most prestigious business magazines. Armed with this acceptance, Fisher decided to press the issue.

While his book editor was doing her job, Fisher asked if she would also teach him something else very important — how to write. He wanted to become a regular contributor to *Forbes*, and after the book editor worked with him, Fisher had lunch with Jim Michaels to explore the possibility.

"Michaels said that I should come back to him with some ideas for columns in the magazine," Fisher says. "I had three columns in my pocket. I took the first one out and let him read it, and he said it was pretty lousy. So I took out another one, and it didn't work either. I took out a third, and he wasn't crazy about it. But he didn't know if maybe I had 20 or 30 of them in my pocket, and this could go on all day. So he agreed to help me learn how to write a column."

The famed business editor was always receptive to the subject matter Fisher presented to him. And subject matter was most important to Fisher himself. He wasn't insulted when Michaels didn't like his writing style. Fisher was quick to admit that he had a lot to learn. From Michaels, he learned that a column — especially a *Forbes* column — had to be entertaining, educational and profitable for the reader. Through tips, suggestions and opinions, the reader must find some value. There must be a financial upside to reading a *Forbes* column, not just word play.

"I stick my neck out more than many columnists," says Fisher, whose Portfolio Strategy column debuted in 1984. This use of the written word has led to employing many other tools available to cred-

> Fisher believes more experts are needed in the financial field, locally and across the country.

CP'S TOP TOOL: THE WRITTEN WORD

ibility marketers. He has written two more books and numerous articles for other financial publications. And he speaks to business groups throughout the country.

He is also founder, chairman and CEO of Fisher Investments Inc., a multibillion-dollar money management firm serving large corporate and public pension plans, as well as endowments, foundations and high net-worth individuals.

The payoff for his efforts has been huge and consistent over time. Fisher credits his media exposure — especially his *Forbes* column — for generating a large chunk of his investment business.

"We started out in 1973 as a small shop doing investments for individuals," he says. "Then we shifted our emphasis to the large pension funds. I credit the media work I've done for the existence of our retail (high net-worth individual) investment arm. Many individual investors wouldn't be with us without the *Forbes* column in particular."

Fisher uses his *Forbes* connection to promote his services in letters to prospective customers for his private client group. "I'm an internationally recognized investment expert who's written three best-selling investment books," the letter claims. "I've been the Portfolio Strategy columnist for *Forbes* for the last 16 years. And my firm, Fisher Investments, Inc., manages over $5 billion for corporations, foundations and individuals." See Appendix C for a full text of the letter.

In financial circles, being a columnist for *Forbes* is almost like having a title such as "baron" or "knight." The Forbes name opens doors for Fisher at major corporations and business groups. He gets invited to speak at conferences, and when his company puts on seminars where he is speaking, the room is full of prospective clients.

"I write for other business publications," Fisher says, "but I never cheapen the currency of *Forbes*. I won't write for publications that don't have credibility, and I won't be a regular columnist for anyone else. Those aren't *Forbes* rules. They are mine, but I think they are prudent."

Fisher believes the opportunities for success with Credibility Power are virtually unlimited in his field because so many people want investment advice. "Today, there are a fair number of big financial journals out there," he says. "If you do an interesting article for them, they will ask for more."

Many of the nation's media markets have local experts — stockbrokers, money managers or college professors — who dispense business advice and commentary with emphasis on the industries or specific businesses that are most important to people in that market.

Fisher believes anyone wanting to provide this type of commentary should decide at the outset whether to concentrate on national or regional publications. "It's much more difficult to go from writing for local publications to a national stage," he explains. "If you want to eventually go national, you should go straight to the national media. Once you are doing national work, you have the credibility to go anywhere you like."

> **Businesspeople often need help learning how to write and use the media.**

Fisher says everybody must do his or her homework to be successful at media work. While there are many top-notch businesspeople, few are trained in use of media.

"Most normal business types are not good writers," he says. "We need help from people who can either write for us or teach us how to write. As long as we understand that, the process will work."

CP'S TOP TOOL: THE WRITTEN WORD

Traditional Book Publishing

We talk about "producing" books these days because standard terms like "write" or "publish" often don't explain what is required to make a book happen. Entry into the book world is far more varied than in years past, when book publishing was more formalized and writers were more at the mercy of the big publishing houses.

Back then, a prospective author usually had to have writing or academic experience. Most authors started out as newspaper reporters, college professors, advertising professionals or public relations practitioners. Today, anyone with the talent and inclination can produce a book.

The process of submitting books or book ideas has not really changed from the "good old days." From the germ of an idea, an author crafted an outline, then chapters of a book. The prospective author sent the outline and three chapters to a literary agent. Successful agents lived and worked in New York City.

All the major publishing houses were headquartered within a small area in Manhattan. It was conceivable that an agent could visit every major editor on behalf of the author in an afternoon, but things never went this quickly. Sometimes months or even years passed before action was taken on a manuscript.

Many books were rejected because they dealt with themes foreign to the urban sensibilities of the editors. Books thought to be too regional were relegated to the academic presses that operated from universities all across the nation. Today, small publishing houses of all types accept those marginal books.

Decades ago, the bottom line didn't always dictate which books saw the light of day. Sometimes editors accepted work that especially intrigued them from authors they respected, even though they knew the books had little commercial appeal and probably wouldn't turn a profit.

Once the editors accepted a project, book pages flew back and forth between author and editor for correction and rewrite. The publishing house usually gave the author an advance payment that was offset by royalties on the sale of books. In most cases the agent kept 10 to 20 percent of all payments to the author as his or her compensation.

The time period from the completion of the manuscript until finished books hit the store shelves was from nine to 18 months. During that time, a cover was designed, quotes gathered for the book jacket and a plan finalized for the promotion and distribution of the book. Publishers decided how many books to print and bind and they paid all the expenses of the venture.

When the book was printed, the publisher sold copies to a distribution company, which resold them directly to the bookstores. Bookstores were the only place you went to purchase a book, and they were the only source of revenue from the sale of books.

Before the book was released, the public relations department of the publishing house decided how to promote the book. They began by distributing unprinted proofs of the book to newspaper and magazine editors all over the country. The publisher paid for tours of strategic cities, with book signings, newspaper interviews and television and radio appearances.

Books were made available as the promotion was rolled out, to achieve maximum sales during the relatively short time when "buzz" was created about the book.

After a few weeks of intense cooperation between the publisher and the author, most of the promotional activities would be over. The publisher would assess the commercial viability of the book. If the book had taken hold in the marketplace, a steady stream of sales resulted. At some point, the publisher decided whether a second printing, or even an updated edition of the book, was a commercial possibility.

The New Book Business

In the past decade, the consolidation of publishing concerns into a few very large companies owned by even larger corporate interests has produced dramatic changes in the book business.

From the publishing example above, these steps are the same as they were in the good old days.

- Agents still represent authors, and they perform that service for 10 to 20 percent of all royalties.
- Authors whose books are accepted by a major publishing house receive an advance on royalties. Such advances average 20 to 50 percent of the estimated total royalties expected from the book.
- The publishing process still takes nine to 18 months from finished manuscript to books on the shelf. This schedule can be compressed for books with timely content.
- The publisher still pays all expenses.
- The publisher still controls how many books are printed, when reprints occur, how books are distributed and how much promotion is undertaken.

The difference today is that publishing — like most businesses — is totally controlled by bottom-line considerations. An author is not published because an editor likes his or her style or sees something in that author's work that might result in sales down the line. The large publishing houses must believe that a book will sell a certain number of copies in a short amount of time, or it will never be published.

This preoccupation with the bottom line has brought about the era of celebrity writers, in which the name of the author is often larger on the cover than the book's title. The author's name often makes the sale, whether or not the book is worthy.

Singer-songwriter Jimmy Buffett is a good example of the celebrity author. The cover of his first nonfiction book, *A Pirate Looks at Fifty*, contains not one but two very prominent uses of his name, along with a photo of Buffett on a beach. All three elements are displayed more prominently than the book's title, which recalls one of Buffett's hit recordings.

Buffett has not had a hit song since Jimmy Carter was president, but he plays to sold-out concert crowds all across the country every summer. His fans, called parrotheads, come to his concerts dressed in tropical attire and ready to party. They sing along with Buffett's classic tunes and are tremendously loyal.

> **Before publishing a book today, you should assess the work's commercial possibilities.**

On the CBS newsmagazine *60 Minutes*, Buffett explained how that loyalty works into his marketing plan. Always the pragmatist, he figured that if he could sell books to 10 percent of his hard-core fan base, he would have a bestseller. The plan has worked with his two novels, *Tales from Margaritaville* and *Where Is Joe Merchant?*, as well as with the nonfiction book. All of these books have made the *New York Times* list.

A practical assessment of the size of the market is valuable to any author. But most of us aren't celebrities or one of the handful of prolific, best-selling authors like John Grisham, Michael Crichton or

CP'S TOP TOOL: THE WRITTEN WORD

Danielle Steele, whose books are churned out by the major publishing houses. Our place may not be with one of the large publishers, but there is a place for us.

In fact, the merger-and-acquisition frenzy in the book business has created a multi-tiered publishing industry that produces more books than ever before and affords a writer more opportunity to publish.

The top tier of publishing still includes the big houses, many of which are still headquartered in New York City. The next tier is a cottage industry of small and intermediate-sized publishers that fill the vacuum left by consolidation of many large companies.

These smaller publishers are located all over the country. They've registered successes handling books the large houses would not consider. While the large publishers are looking for million-selling blockbusters, the smaller companies can thrive on books that sell as few as 10,000 copies.

As publishers have dispersed around the country, literary agents have followed them. Agents don't just walk down a busy Manhattan street to do business anymore. An agent in New Jersey recently told us about his attempt to pitch a project to a book editor in Seattle who works on a freelance basis for a publisher headquartered in Dallas. These attempts are still based on personal relationships. But today, the relationships are carried on via telephone, FedEx, fax and e-mail instead of during three-martini lunches.

Doing business with this new breed of agent and publisher can be disconcerting. One writer told about a surprise visit he made to the publishing house that contracted to produce his book. The book editor bragged to the writer over the telephone about the view of greenbelt out his office window. Having never been there before, the writer envisioned a large corporate headquarters, perhaps overlooking a golf course. What he found on his surprise visit was the editor's modest home, his bedroom office and the view of a kids' soccer field.

"The publishing business is an illusion," says author Don Sanders. He and his wife, Susan, produced an illustrated book, *The American Drive-In Movie Theatre*, in 1997. They presented the work to numerous agents and editors before getting a positive response from Motorbooks International, which publishes books relating to the automobile.

"We kept telling the Motorbooks people that we wanted to come to their place, to sit down and discuss the book," Sanders says. "They said that wouldn't be necessary, that we could do it all by mail or fax. But we'd been deceived by other publishers. We wanted to make sure they were actually who and where they said they were. They were shocked when we actually visited them. No writer had ever done that before. But we felt better because they were for real and we knew that for sure."

Today Don and Susan Sanders run the Susan Sanders Agency, which does publicity campaigns for authors of hot new books.

"Very few first-time authors truly understand the publishing world and its complexities," Sanders told *The Dallas Business Journal*. "We wasted three years in pursuit of someone to help us, only to be rebuffed because we were not published. Then we learned the true intricacies of getting a book published, including the fact that we had to help promote the book. We did that successfully and we've been favorably reviewed in national and international newspapers. We learned that you must believe so much in your project that you won't take 'no' for an answer."

When dealing with publishers large and small, ask plenty of questions and get the entire agreement in writing. Especially important are the following:

CP'S TOP TOOL: THE WRITTEN WORD

- Know exactly how much profit the sale of each book will produce. This percentage, known as the royalty, may only amount to about $1 per book payable from the publisher to the author.
- All expenses are the responsibility of the publisher. That's why on a $16 book, the author might get $1 and the publisher takes home the rest.
- The extent of the promotional campaign should be spelled out. Is someone from the promotions department assigned to the project, with authority to schedule events and the experience to handle those duties? Book signings are easy to schedule. Most bookstores want them. But signings without media events supporting them are useless. Radio, television or newspaper reports let people know a signing is scheduled.
- If you believe the initial press run for the book should be 20,000 and the publisher wants to print 3,000, it's clear there is little confidence the book will sell.
- Under what conditions, including sales level, will the publisher order a second printing?

Case History:
Can One Book Be Like Another?

Dr. Allen Perlis has been a teacher most of his life. For more than 25 years, he taught at the university level and won numerous awards for teaching excellence. As chairman of the English department at the University of Alabama–Birmingham, he earned praise in academic circles for his books of literary criticism.

CREDIBILITY POWER

Perlis got his real estate license and began to sell houses in the late 1980s. By 1990, he was earning more money in real estate each year than he was teaching. Today, he is a full-time broker who has sold almost 1,000 homes in the Birmingham area.

And still he approaches his work as a teacher would, informing buyers about the joys of home ownership and the worthiness of certain amenities and areas of town. In 1999, he was asked to contribute to a series of books published by the large publishing house IDG Books Worldwide. This is the house that publishes the enormously successful series of instructional books *...for Dummies.*

"They were looking for someone with publishing credentials and they made contact with me through a small local publisher who is familiar with my work," Perlis says.

The result was *The Unofficial Guide to Buying A Home*, written by Perlis and edited by his wife, educator and writer Beth Bradley. The book has sold more than 40,000 copies nationwide and added credibility in real estate sales to the extensive résumé of the former college professor.

"The book has allowed me to use my academic reputation to sell myself as a real estate professional," Perlis says. It has also given him nationwide recognition.

"I have gotten some customers locally from the book," he says, "but most of the people who've come to me are relocating to the Birmingham area. They are people from around the country who read the book. To them, I am the expert in Birmingham real estate."

CP'S TOP TOOL: THE WRITTEN WORD

Self-Publishing

A third tier of the book publishing business — and the fastest growing — is self-publishing. The rise of the small publisher, along with the growth of desktop publishing, has allowed many people to publish their own books. Writing a great book may require intellect, but publishing one is mostly an organizational undertaking.

Following are some practical suggestions for making self-publishing a success:

Make your book an appealing package

Learn about the book business simply by entering a Barnes & Noble or one of the other large chain bookstores and looking at the books on display. Just stand near the front door for a moment and scan the shelves, detecting the books that have the greatest eye appeal from this distance. Then move into the store and look more closely at several of those books. See what makes them stand out from the others. Note the use of color, type, photography and illustration. Often it is possible to piece together a memorable book jacket by appropriating (read "stealing") ideas from one book cover or another. Most book designers do exactly the same thing. While surveying the shelves, you will notice many book jackets with similar graphic elements.

Make the book title short, simple and memorable

A great title introduces the book to the reader. It must catch the prospective reader's attention and tell what the book is about. The title must roll off the tongue of reviewers and media types who might interview you about the book. It must be easy for prospective buyers and bookstore employees to remember. The first 30 characters of the title must identify the book easily, since many bookstore computer systems allow you to enter only that number of characters to conduct a search. Computer searches are based on the use of keywords. To make your title memorable, you should begin your title with a memorable keyword.

Test this by searching Amazon.com, BN.com or one of the other book databases through the use of this keyword. For instance, when we were discussing possible titles for this book, we narrowed our search to "Credibility Power" and one of several titles that begin with "How to…." Amazon.com showed only a handful of books beginning with the word "credibility," as opposed to hundreds that begin with "how-to." Imagine how much easier and more productive it is to ask a bookstore employee for that book about credibility than that how-to book.

Establish a book imprint that sounds like a real entity

The book imprint is the name of your publishing company. This name is printed on the spine of the book and on the copyright page. Most publishing companies have either "Books," "Press," or "Publishing" as part of the name. The imprint should reflect the types of books being published. Some publishing companies utilize more than one imprint. They might publish business books under, say, BIZ Books, and children's literature under Duck Quacker Press.

Each book must have its own International Standard Book Number (ISBN) and bar code

All books sold through bookstores must have an ISBN. This is like a social security number for the book. Without an ISBN, prospective customers and bookstore personnel cannot find the book. For each publishing imprint, apply for an ISBN Publisher Prefix. This prefix can be registered by writing to R.R. Bowker, 121 Chanlon Road, New Providence, New Jersey 07974 or online at www.bowkerlink.com. Bowker will assign several 10-digit numbers for use on your books. To be accepted for sale in most bookstores, the book must also include a bar code that store employees can scan for ISBN and price. A list of Bookland EAN bar code film master suppliers can be obtained from Bowker.

Register with Books In Print and the Library of Congress

Once the ISBN is assigned for a book, obtain an Advance Book Information (ABI) form by writing R.R. Bowker's Data Collection Center, P.O. Box 6000-0103, Oldsmar, Florida 34677-0103. After the title is selected, fill out the form and send it back to Bowker. Completing this form registers the book with Books In Print (BIP). Most bookstores update their own computerized ordering systems with information from BIP. The book is not listed with Books In Print until the completed ABI form is returned to Bowker.

Also, register the book with the Library of Congress. Many libraries will order the book based on it being listed in the Library of Congress catalog. Fill out a Request for Preassignment of Library of Congress Catalog Card Number. This can be obtained by writing Library of Congress, Cataloging in Publication Division, 101 Independence Ave., S.E., Washington, D.C. 20540-4320.

Send out review copies well in advance of publication

Newspaper and magazine reviewers sometimes need several months to fit a book into their schedule. When the manuscript is finalized, even before printing, send review copies straight off the word processor. The book editors of most magazines and large-city newspapers will not review self-help or regional books. Many have space for only the most outstanding new fiction and an occasional nonfiction work of great substance by a well-known author.

Many of these publications review books in other sections, such as the lifestyle pages or the business section. Prepare a cover letter that asks the book editor to forward the book to the appropriate person if it is not right for the book section. Hand-deliver the manuscript to the book editor of your local paper.

Local writers often get more consideration. For those copies that must be mailed, go to the post office and pick up a supply of Priority Mailboxes used to mail videotapes. These packets hold most books 6 inches by 9 inches or smaller, along with reviews, cover letters and other information. The boxes are free. Slap a Priority Mail stamp on each box and it is ready to go.

Consider hiring a well-known local journalist to write a sample review under his or her own byline

Send the book and the sample review to a mailing list of newspaper book editors. Contact information is available through such listings as the All-In-One Media Directory published by Gebbie Press, P.O. Box 1000, New Paltz, New York 12561 or online at www.gebbieinc.com. Also available is Burrelle's Media Directory online at www.burrelles.com. Without one of these lists, it will be necessary to call newspapers to verify name, title and mailing address.

Even after sending the book to an editor, bombard that editor with reviews or stories from other papers as they are written. If other journalists write about the book, editors will realize its importance.

CP'S TOP TOOL: THE WRITTEN WORD

Secure endorsements in the form of book-jacket quotes from the most famous or well-connected people available

Business guru Tom Peters assured the success of his bestseller *In Search of Excellence* through a unique strategy. He and co-author Bob Waterman wrote about some of the largest and most successful companies in the nation. They covered the companies they liked, making what they wrote highly laudatory. CEOs, board members and consultants with ties to these companies were eager to supply testimonials to a book that praised many of their efforts. When the book was published, many of the companies purchased multiple copies for employees and other important people. Many well-known people are approached every day to endorse one thing or the other. Zig Zilgar says he is asked to write several book-jacket quotes each week. Use any method available to secure testimonials and endorsements. This is the time to ask for help from friends and associates.

Distribute the book through a reputable company and not from the trunk of a car

Distribution is often an afterthought, but it is one of the most important parts of the publishing process, considering the author's need to sell copies of the book to recoup costs.

Self-publishing a book costs you money upfront. You are paying the fees and charges that a large publisher would pay in the conventional publishing process.

You may go into this process feeling that it's OK for your book to be a loss leader. But by the time you've paid to have the book designed, edited, printed and bound, recovering that money may be important to you.

Most books don't make it into the bookstores without help from a wholesaler or distributor. Chain-store buyers hate to deal directly with small publishers. They want to deal with businesses that supply them with many different books. That way, ordering, shipping and accounting are more organized. Terms of sale are known. They only have to write one check instead of dealing with numerous invoices.

Finding a dependable distributor can be a nightmare. Two large wholesalers, Baker & Taylor and Ingram, handle books of all types nationwide. But these large companies don't handle small publishers very well.

PSG Books is a small publisher of trade paperbacks caught in a Catch-22 while trying to work with Ingram. Although Ingram has a special division that handles small-press issues, the company refused to stock any of PSG's books. When an employee at Barnes & Noble called up any of the titles, his in-store system indicated they were on back order. But the policy of B&N and many other stores is to decline to back-order books. So the system kicked out the order, saying they were either unavailable or out of print.

Many other large wholesaler/distributors will accept books from a small publisher only if there is a demand. But the system will express a demand only if there are books in stock. What is wrong with this picture?

Since most small publishers aren't in a position to lobby the top executives of Ingram or Baker & Taylor, the only recourse is to deal with smaller distributors who specialize in certain types of books or service only a portion of the country. By searching the Internet for book distributors, the owner of PSG Books found a distributor with several warehouse facilities. The small distributor stocked the books and shipped them to stores as promotional efforts created demand. New issue catalogs are not widely distributed, but at least they handle the books.

CP'S TOP TOOL: THE WRITTEN WORD

Be clear on financial arrangements with a distributor

A distributor expects to retain 55 to 60 percent of the cover price and pay you the remaining 40 to 45 percent of the cover price for each book sold. Publishers usually pay to ship books to the distributor, while the distributor absorbs the cost of shipping to bookstores. Bookstores receive deep discounts from the distributor to entice them to order the book, so the distributor retains a greater percentage than the publisher does. Say the book has a cover price of $16.95. The publisher receives between $6.78 and $7.62 per book.

A $16.95 book that sells 10,000 copies will pay the publisher a gross income of $67,800 to $76,200.

This may seem like a lot of money, but remember that the publisher must pay all of the expenses. That includes the promotion necessary to interest people in buying the book. Under a conventional publishing arrangement, the publisher pays all these expenses, gets most of the money and gives the author about a dollar a book.

Payments from the distributor to the publisher are due 90 days following the month that the book is sold, and the book is subject to being returned unsold by the store for a full year. For instance, a book that sells in December is tallied at the end of the month and payment is made the following April.

Remember that distributors are simply fulfillment houses. They do not create demand. They do not promote the book except in catalogs of their titles. They do want to hear about promotional efforts, so they can anticipate demand.

Print a substantial quantity of books

The number of books to print is an important consideration. Printing novices always ask for some magical printing cutoff, a mystical number where costs per copy are suddenly very low. In truth, there is no magic number. The number of books to print is based merely on the idea of how many books will sell. If the book is regional, it may not sell more than a few thousand copies. A national book on a subject of wide interest may sell 15,000 to 25,000 copies. Find out how similar books have sold and this will give a good indication of the printing needs. Print the greatest number of copies possible in the first printing. This will keep you from having to do a quick second printing and is the most cost-effective way to proceed.

Use high quality paper, the best graphic treatments and as much color as possible

High production values help to sell a book. By perusing the bookstores, you can see the books that stand out on the shelves. Those are the ones with full-color covers, nice paper and the use of graphic elements on the inside pages.

Get several printing bids

Many printers around the country specialize in book printing. Obtain bids from several printers based on the type of book (softcover, hardback, etc.), size of the book (height and width), number of pages, type of paper, use of graphics inside and use of color on the cover.

Begin to promote even before books are delivered

The book's publication date should be at least a couple of months later than the delivery date from the printer. For instance, if books are expected in October, date the book for the following year. The media

CP'S TOP TOOL: THE WRITTEN WORD

and the public want a product that is new and up to date. While the book is being printed, prepare press releases for the local media and begin to schedule events.

Always begin a promotional campaign in your home city

Schedule one or more book signings by calling the special events coordinator or promotions director at prominent bookstores in the area. Dealing with bookstore personnel can be one of the most pleasant parts of this process. Most are eager to showcase authors and books for their customers. Many will send out invitations to attract people to the store. Invite any potential customers to such an event, and mention the book signings in any press releases to local media.

Credibility marketers with plenty of extra cash use the initial book signings exclusively to attract attention to their work. One author who is very well known in his hometown staged his first book signing at a local Barnes & Noble and contributed his portion of the profits to the local charity. The signing became a party for his family and friends, as well as several business associates. Besides attracting a good crowd, this gesture generated large amounts of publicity in media throughout the area.

Prepare a media kit and let it grow over the course of the campaign

The media kit may begin with a press release, a sample review and a copy of the book. Add tear sheets from other news stories as well as copies of the bookstore invitation, mention of the author in the store's newsletter and a list of questions reporters might ask the author. These questions may be those asked by customers at the book signings. Every mention of the book or the author in the media adds credibility.

CREDIBILITY POWER

Book signings in prominent bookstores should anchor city tours

Book signings rarely sell many books. Look at them as marketing opportunities. Once a book signing is scheduled, call newspaper, radio and television reporters and editors. Tell them, "I will be in the area on this date, if you would like to interview me." The immediacy of this approach often attracts the local media. For the credibility marketing practitioner, a book signing in another city can be an excuse to invite people you otherwise would not meet. These people might include potential customers, competitors or members of the media.

Constantly re-evaluate the campaign

A multi-city promotional campaign costs time and money. Make a commitment to see it through, but evaluate the campaign at critical junctures. Do sales or publicity justify the cost of the campaign? Keep the book's distributor aware of the campaign. Give him several weeks' lead time to get books to stores where you are promoting.

Purchase the most important book on self-publishing and seek out all the information you can

The first step every author should take is to pick up *The Complete Guide to Self-Publishing* by Tom and Marilyn Ross. This book is a 400-page reference work with more about book self-publishing than you will ever want to know. Read this book from cover to cover before beginning the process.

Co-author Marilyn Ross is also executive director of the Small Publishers Association of North America. This organization offers resources to help small publishers produce worthwhile books, along with marketing information and links to related groups. Contact the Small Publishers Association of North America at P.O. Box 1306, Buena Vista, Colorado 81211 and online at www.spannet.org.

Case History:
Given the Choice, He'll Publish Himself

Benjamin Kaplan is the type of bright young author that major publishers love. His nonfiction book, *How to Go to College Almost for Free: The Secrets of Winning Scholarship Money* sold well and he plans a full line of books, audio and videotapes and electronic reports.

But Kaplan is not the darling of the New York publishing houses. Instead, he has formed his own company, Waggle Dancer Books, and is publishing the books and other media products himself.

"What I like about self-publishing is that if you succeed, you succeed on your own merits," Kaplan tells *The New York Times*. And succeed he has, becoming a talk show and bookstore favorite after receiving almost $90,000 in scholarship money and writing his 316-page book.

A Harvard graduate with a degree in economics, Kaplan finished the book while living with his parents during the summer of 1999. He formatted the entire book himself on his computer, while his parents helped with the editing. And they contracted with a printer for 5,000 copies of the book, paying the bill with money from Kaplan's unused college fund. Kaplan then began a relentless promotional campaign of high school appearances and book signings, then television and radio guest spots. After selling 25,000 copies in the first six months, he convinced wholesaler Ingram as well as distributors Amazon.com and Baker & Taylor to pick up his book.

Self-publishing is nothing new for many successful books, such as *The Celestine Prophecy* and *The Christmas Box*. Impressive sales of these books in the early stages gained the attention of major publishers, who offered the authors substantial contracts. The same thing happened to Kaplan, but this shrewd young author/entrepreneur turned down all offers.

Most young authors would be grateful to have major publishers pursuing them, but Kaplan is looking for something more. He wants partnerships in tune with his desire to provide books and other materials that help families through certain milestones, such as college and high school. He believes the most important factor is not literary talent, but the willingness to work hard shaping a letter or preparing book shipments with foam filler.

"Stephen King, Michael Crichton and John Grisham are all great authors," Kaplan says. "But I can pack books in peanuts better than anyone."

Newsletter Concept

Marketers who use the written word can also generate credibility power in a newsletter. When Clint David looked for ways to distinguish his law firm from others, he decided to publish a newsletter. His firm had purchased advertising in the business press, and he had a brochure. David liked the advantages of publishing a newsletter. He could control what was said about the firm, target distribution of the information and get the information to clients and potential clients more quickly and at a lower cost than with many other methods.

Not everyone in the firm favored a newsletter. Several attorneys said they received newsletters from clients and other law firms, and they didn't read any of them. They wondered what percentage of the

CP'S TOP TOOL: THE WRITTEN WORD

newsletters they printed wound up in the "circular file."

The firm's communications consultant agreed that many newsletters get thrown away. But some of them do not and others are read before they go into the can. He explained that a newsletter published independently of any other media might not be worth the money. His idea was that newsletter stories should be the basis for articles submitted to other media.

The first issue of the David, Goodman & Madole newsletter consisted of the following stories:

- Agreements between employers and employees that the employee who leaves the company will not get a job competing against it for a specified time
- Dram shop laws, which govern the sale of alcoholic beverages
- A survey about what people dislike about attorneys
- The Good Works Case of the Month, the story of how the law firm recovered an heirloom for an elderly relative of one of the firm's employees

> **Most newsletter stories should be informative enough that the local media will want to reprint them.**

The stories were short, to the point and written in a personal style. They represented different areas of the law. And perhaps most importantly, they were timely. The first newsletter was published between the Thanksgiving and Christmas holidays. Timeliness made it potentially valuable for other forms of promotion.

CREDIBILITY POWER

The idea of the newsletter is to take a story the media is already reporting and apply your own expertise to the subject matter. This is called finding a news "peg" or "slant."

The firm's expert in employment law wrote the story on employment agreements with the help of the consultant. His story centered on the case of a local television newscaster who had left one station and was covered by an agreement not to compete against his old employer for a certain time. He was scheduled to make his first on-air appearance for his new employer in the next month. Neither the attorney who wrote the story nor anyone else in the firm was personally involved in this case in any way. But this well-known and timely case served as the basis of an article about how non-compete agreements are necessary tools for many types of businesses.

Besides using the article in the newsletter, the consultant sent it to the local business journal, which ran it on the commentary page.

The story on dram shop laws was also timely, with holiday parties about to begin. This article was sent to the editor of the lifestyle sec-

Newsletters often serve a dual purpose. Some businesses use their publications as the basis for stories they place in the local media. In this way, they leverage one Credibility Power venture into another.

tion of the local newspaper. The editor included comments from the story in an article about playing it safe while serving alcohol at seasonal get-togethers.

By alertly combining their efforts with those already in the news, the attorneys created effective promotional efforts by leveraging one medium into another.

Newsletter Production

Producing a newsletter is not difficult. Anyone with the tools of desktop publishing — a computer, laser printer and scanner — can bring a newsletter to life. Producing a newsletter that looks and reads professionally enough to warrant use of the articles in other media may require the services of a designer and a writer/editor.

Many of the most effective newsletters are graphically interesting and clever in the writing and presentation of articles. Newsletters are very personal displays of your expertise, and they often generate Credibility Power. Newsletters like this mirror the personalities of the people producing them. If a newsletter is fun, clever and interesting, the recipient will come away feeling that the people who produced it also possess those qualities.

Language and graphics combine to present an image of the newsletter and its creators at the same time. Use of jargon and splashes of color convey less formality or a sense of humor. If you see your customers as stiff and formal, heavy paper, muted colors and formal language may appeal to them.

Newsletters should be produced at least three or four times a year, on a regular schedule. They should be mailed to a mailing list that is constantly updated by correcting names, titles and addresses.

CREDIBILITY POWER

Media Relations

As long as reporters have been writing about the activities of citizens, some of those citizens have been manipulating what the media says about them.

In politics, media manipulation even has a name. It's called *spin*. The important thing may be not what you actually say, but the spin or interpretation that public relations people put on your remarks.

PR people have been manipulating the media in this way for the past half-century. This manipulation has increased as cities become larger and reporters can no longer know all the good stories available to them without help. There are also more media people needing to fill space or broadcast time with such stories.

When you read a mostly positive newspaper or magazine feature about a person or company, it's a good bet that a public relations person presented the idea to an editor or reporter. When you see an investigative story or feature that's critical of a person or company, a PR rep experienced in crisis media management probably worked hard to influence the writer and make the story appear less threatening.

There are many ways to use the media to enhance Credibility Power, such as:

- Convincing an editor or reporter to write a newspaper or magazine story or produce a broadcast segment on a particular area of expertise
- Convincing those same editors or reporters to allow you to contribute a segment on a particular subject area
- Selling the editors on employing you for such segments on a regular basis

CP'S TOP TOOL: THE WRITTEN WORD

- Becoming a regular source of information when reporters compile stories on your area of expertise
- Convincing an investigative reporter that your product or service is good for the community and shouldn't be criticized

Many people labor under the misconception that because public relations people know media people personally, they are better able to manipulate them than CP practitioners. That may be true in general, but it isn't always the case. Some media people realize they are being manipulated and they don't want to talk to PR people. Other media people know that PR reps can often do them a real service, and they welcome their input.

What all media people want are very good story ideas. Some PR representatives are valuable because they started their careers in journalism and know a good story when they see one. Unless the stories are based on good ideas, most decent journalists will not run them — even to benefit their good friends.

CHAPTER 9

IN THIS CHAPTER
- Public Speaking
- Seminars and Workshops
- Audiocassettes/Videotapes/Software
- Radio and Television
- Paid Programming

Other Tools for Cashing In

Use of the written word can evolve into other products and services that can elevate an expert's status to that of trusted authority. Take a look at some other tools used to display Credibility Power.

OTHER TOOLS FOR CASHING IN

CREDIBILITY PROFILE

Dr. Mark Bernstien had modest goals when he began to offer seminars for women interested in his obstetrics and gynecology practice. By keeping his expectations in check, he is successful using the power of credibility.

You can be successful at credibility marketing on many different levels. Not everyone will write a best-selling book or make millions of dollars filling stadiums with people anxious to hear their every word. Other businesspeople have quite modest, attainable goals for their Credibility Power ventures.

At its most elemental level, CP can enhance the core businesses of already successful people. That's how Dr. Mark Bernstien views his use of seminars and a newsletter about his practice. For many years, they have drawn additional OB-GYN patients to him.

Bernstien is a member of a small medical practice operating from a large urban hospital. He and his partners understand the many advantages of even the most rudimentary marketing efforts.

"You don't just open your doors to a completely full practice," says Bernstien. "You've got to educate patients, cater to their needs and provide services to make them want to continue to visit you."

For many years, the practice has sponsored seminars on women's health issues. The seminars are held in the hospital cafeteria six times a year. About 200 people attend each session, including existing patients, their friends and relatives and women who may be shopping for a new OB-GYN doctor.

CREDIBILITY POWER

"The seminars help us to maintain our patient base plus get new patients," Bernstien explains. "Our patients talk to other women about the seminars. The other women say, 'My doctor never does that; maybe I'll switch.' It's hard to quantify the number of patients we get from the seminars, but I know they are successful."

Because the seminars are educational, Bernstien believes they serve the practice in other ways: "We believe informed patients are better patients. They take better care of themselves. And I don't have to say the same thing a hundred times a day because so many of our patients come to the seminars and have their questions answered."

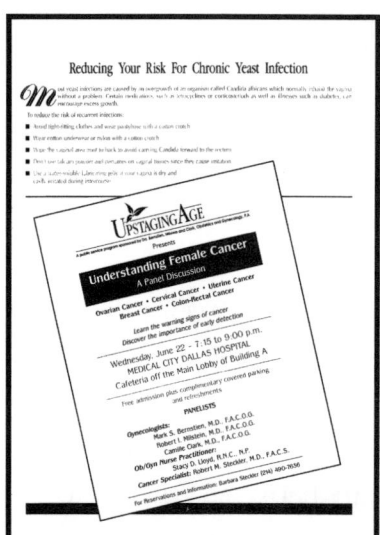

In Bernstien's case, paid advertising is part of credibility marketing. His practice and the hospital jointly pay to place ads in the local newspaper announcing the seminars. The hospital also mails out copies of his newsletter.

"When people from the hospital see us with 200 people in their cafeteria, they know we are attracting patients who will use the hospital's services," Bernstien says. "They like what we're doing and so they support us. I'm sure they would support anyone who would do something like this."

Bernstien says he and his partners also gain credibility from the newsletter. Each newsletter publicizes specific seminars to a targeted segment of their 10,000-patient database.

"Say we are doing a seminar on menopause," Bernstien says. "Our computer can pick out the patients who are age 50 or over and selectively target them. Then the hospital sends out several thousand copies to a list of prospective patients. That's how we get new people to attend."

Public Speaking

An ideal way to exploit your expertise is by speaking in public about a specific field of work. The opportunities for public speaking are virtually endless. Groups like Toastmasters provide a forum to hone your speaking skills before trying them out on the public.

Every chapter of Kiwanis, Rotary and other service or professional clubs must schedule a speaker each month. The luncheon audience may only be a handful of people, but beginners often find this a great venue for getting comfortable with public speaking and determining whether their core businesses can be helped by such appearances.

Many local associations, nonprofit groups and parent organizations also need speakers. Most of these groups realize that only inexperienced speakers work for no money. These engagements provide a chance to gain experience, leave a few business cards and uncover other speaking opportunities. Numerous speakers' bureaus exist to schedule those with experience. Many trade groups provide speakers who concentrate on a single industry. There are also for-profit bureaus, like the one operated by Dottie and Lilly Walters. Potential speakers pay these bureaus a commission from speaking fees.

Seminars and Workshops

Education is the currency used to spread expertise to a waiting public, and there is no better way to educate people than face-to-face during a seminar or workshop. Experts in many fields sponsor free seminars that educate people about an area of interest while showcasing their abilities. The title of the seminar or workshop is typically "how to" followed by virtually any activity that will save or make people money or contribute to their general well being.

Among the secrets to a successful seminar or workshop are:

Select a winning topic

Nothing is more defeating than planning a public event ... and the public doesn't show up. People have many meaningful ways to spend their time. Just because a seminar is free doesn't mean that people will attend. If the topic is money, the content of the seminar must provide a way to earn or save more. If the discussion centers on self-improvement, you may have to work hard to make your advice new and improved. If the talk will delve into leisure time activities, try to make it fun and worthwhile.

Consider the team approach

The element most likely to draw a crowd is a famous speaker. Since most of us are average folks, we're better off bringing in other experts and bowling the people over with expertise. For instance, a financial planner presenting a seminar on retirement planning might team up with an expert on life insurance or long-term care. Besides doubling the universe of possible participants, this approach gives the opportunity to share the work and expenses as well as the anxiety of putting on a public event.

Spend time in preparation

Remember that Zig Ziglar practices three to five hours for each

Examples of seminar topics that could be taught by individuals profiled in this book might include how to:

- Stay fit and healthy
- Set an elegant table
- Get divorced and remain friends
- Be the service guru of an industry
- Control pests and be environmentally friendly
- Defeat hate groups
- Become an internationally known speaker
- Grow flowering plants year-round
- Concentrate on what matters most in life
- Sell more in less time
- Make the most of your gifts
- Serve God and country
- Profit from professional sports
- Stop creditor harassment
- Be the best you can be
- Nurture ideas and sprout success
- Have the proper attitude
- Make the most of your investments
- Craft a best-selling book
- Win custody of your children
- Deal with women's health issues

speech, even after all these years. If the goal of the seminar is to increase your core business, here's the best possible opportunity to bring all those potential customers together in one place, listening only to you. Don't blow it by arriving unprepared.

Prepare well in advance

Besides allowing adequate time to prepare, you must consider the time needed for promotion to reach potential seminar attendees and for them to respond. Before setting a date for the event, prepare a timeline, working backward with realistic deadlines and a reservoir of time for events not under your control. Those would include time for mail to reach possible participants and for them to respond.

The important events along this timeline include:

- Point at which seminar is fully prepared
- Deadline to reserve seminar space
- Time to prepare brochure, mailer or ad promoting seminar
- Date for brochure mailing or ad placement
- Time for potential attendees to respond
- Deadline for response
- Time for follow-up confirmation
- Time to rerun ad, mail out additional material or seek third-party help to attract participants

Offer incentives

Preparation of a seminar or workshop involves more than just learning a script. For the first event like this, you are simply throwing yourself in front of the public, hoping to attract attendees and not lose money. Think about offering incentives that add comfort as well as value, and promote them in all literature about the event. Serving breakfast or lunch adds to the comfort factor. Consider giving away door prizes such as gift certificates to restaurants or hotels. First-timers might give away a set of materials from Ziglar or another well-known speaker. Sometimes a business sponsoring your seminar will provide these prizes free or at low cost for their promotional value.

Know when to charge for a seminar

Gauge the value of the seminar material to attendees. Many people do seminars solely to attract clients who can increase the core business. With that goal in mind, a seminar that costs you money to present becomes an acceptable business expense. As you gain experience, your presentation may become more dynamic and original, and it may become easier to attract paying attendees. At this point, the law of supply and demand comes into play. What began as an exercise in promoting an existing business may evolve into a business all its own.

This magic point, when you slap an admission price on the brochure and kick the promotion into a higher gear, must be approached with calm resolve. The ego involvement of having a roomful of people hang on your every word must not overtake reality. Is the message compelling, interesting and valuable enough that people will pay $49 or $99 or $189 to attend? Separate the value of the product from the fun of the moment.

A service that costs money is perceived as more valuable than something that is given away. Ask yourself if the product being presented to people is worth the asking price. Is it original and effective? Would you pay to attend? You want to cross the gulf between offering a free seminar and requiring payment for one at the correct time.

CREDIBILITY POWER

Be creative about promotion

An inexpensive flyer or direct-mail piece can promote your seminar. But where do you send it?

Compile a list of clients, potential clients, associates, vendors and anyone else who might have an interest in the topic or know someone who does. Obtain a list of potential attendees from a local association or consider renting one from a company that sells mailing lists.

An association may sell a membership directory. The names in this directory will have to be typed into a word processing program or scanned into a computerized optical character recognition program.

Mailing list brokers charge for lists, but theirs are the easiest to use. These lists usually cost more than those from an association, but the names and addresses are up-to-date and can be sorted practically any way you like. For a seminar on retirement planning, purchase a list of people in nearby ZIP codes between the ages of 45 and 65 with enough disposable income to need investment advice. Purchase a computerized list for unlimited printing of labels or on labels for one-time use.

Affiliation with a large organization may bring help with the distribution of promotional materials. Dr. Mark Bernstien printed enough newsletters advertising his seminars that his hospital could mail extra copies to prospective patients. The hospital also paid for ads in the local newspaper and provided the hospital cafeteria for the events.

Some large companies provide assistance when the seminar topic benefits employees or the company. For instance, a seminar that could benefit employees might be one on the best use of 401(k) money. Ideas that could benefit the company might be workplace diversity, safety or avoiding sexual harassment lawsuits.

OTHER TOOLS FOR CASHING IN

For a seminar presented to a company population, you may prepare the seminar material and the sponsoring company does the rest. Companies usually send out reminders to the employees, provide rooms for the seminars and offer refreshments. The seminar leader's responsibility is to take a subtle approach to promotion during these seminars. Make certain seminar materials are educational and are not heavy-handed in their promotion of your product or service. It is understood that business will come from employees in exchange for time spent planning the seminar. Just don't abuse the privilege.

Case History:
Leveraging Seminars into Other Credibility Ventures

Ken Bradford has been creating leaders for more than a decade. He began as a part-time instructor for the Dale Carnegie organization when he was employed as an insurance salesman. Then he formulated his own leadership course.

"Carnegie offered a 12-week course with up to 60 people in a class," Bradford says. "We were getting calls from small companies that didn't have that many people and wanted a shorter course. I started doing those classes on the side and it grew into a full-time business."

Bradford pays homage to his Dale Carnegie roots. In fact, his own Leaders Course is "Carnegie" streamlined to its leadership essentials. The course runs one evening a week for six weeks. The materials are succinct, the coursework tightly focused for participants who want to improve their leadership abilities in a short time. In his first eight years, Bradford completed 55 classes and trained 1,400 new leaders. He felt that he was gaining the correct experience to teach any size or variety of training class. Bradford found that just because he was actually doing these classes didn't mean that people would hire him to do more of them.

"I was pitching a software consulting company on doing a seminar for their people," Bradford says. "It was a good-size job. They knew about my classes. People had told them what I could do. But they asked me, 'What have you written?'"

He had spoken a great deal on the subject of leadership, but he hadn't written anything at all. Because of his lack of writing, Bradford didn't get the business. He decided after this rejection to branch out into written materials, writing articles for publications in the speaking field. Soon his ideas began to take shape as a book, *Bradford's 22 Laws of Speaking*. While he and an editor worked on this book, Bradford wrote and published a pocket-size book titled *A Great Little Book on Listening*. This small book — which he gives to each of his students — helps them become more aware of the value of listening over talking.

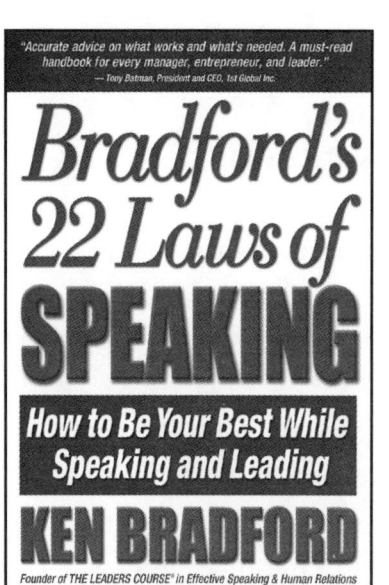

"It's credibility," Bradford notes. "They asked me what I had written, but they wanted to know what makes me credible. College professors are not the only ones who must publish or perish. Public speakers and consultants must write if they want to reach the next level. A book has such credibility that it is considered more important than actually doing what they were hiring me to do."

Bradford understands the symmetry among the various tools that enhance Credibility Power. His course gets him before the public, where word-of-mouth brings him potential clients. And the credibility of the written word often seals the deal.

Audiocassettes/Videotapes/Software

After developing a seminar or writing a book, the logical next step is to commit that material to other media — audiocassette, videotape or CD. Many speakers and seminar leaders give these materials to attendees or have them for back-of-the-room sale.

Case History:
Down a Steep Slope and Around a Learning Curve

Vince Poscente has worked as a motivational speaker since 1995. He has written and self-published a book, *The InVINCEable Principles*, several sets of audiocassettes and a video of one of his high-energy keynote speeches.

Poscente, a Canadian, is a former Olympic speed-skiing record holder, having clocked 135 miles per hour down a steep, icy slope. He speaks on such topics as minimizing risk and achieving peak performance, along with practical approaches to team building and customer service.

Poscente knows the logical extension of your written work is to "put the book on tape. You just break it down into various themes. If the book is good enough to publish, it's good enough for tapes."

Although Poscente knows that writing the book first is more practical, that's not how he did it. He has a four-cassette series titled *Getting Results — New Altitudes for Peak Performance* and one called

CREDIBILITY POWER

Accelerate to Your Objectives. He also has four collections on creating a better life — *Creating Peace of Mind, Creating Balance, Creating Wealth* and *Creating Your Optimum Body*. Each set contains two cassettes.

His video, *A Journey from Ordinary to Extraordinary*, features the speaker in live performance giving a keynote address to a corporate audience.

"This video was pretty easy to do," Poscente says. "I just set up a camera at one of my speeches and gave the tape to an editor when it was over."

Doing audiotapes is a little more involved. "I had to write a script, hire a sound booth and get an editor," he says. "Packaging is important for tapes. I hired a graphic designer to do the packaging and then arranged for distribution."

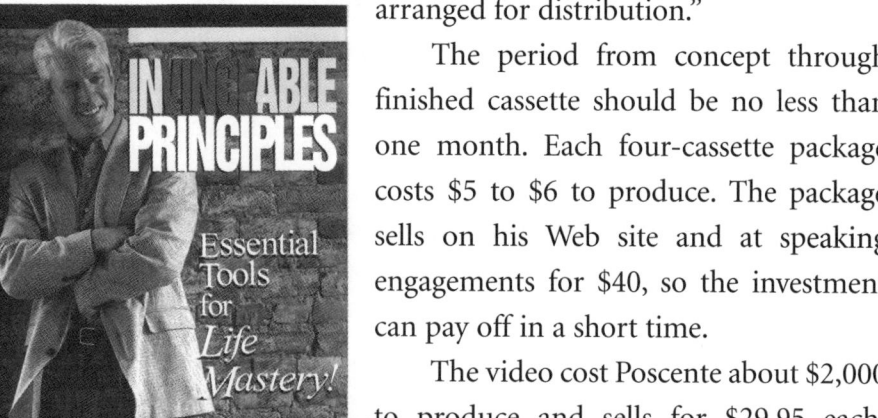

The period from concept through finished cassette should be no less than one month. Each four-cassette package costs $5 to $6 to produce. The package sells on his Web site and at speaking engagements for $40, so the investment can pay off in a short time.

The video cost Poscente about $2,000 to produce and sells for $29.95 each. Offering the same material on CD or DVD could be done for about the same cost.

"These materials are valuable for me to have even if I only sell them at my bookings," he points out. "I speak to about 100,000 people every year, and a good percentage of the people who hear me want something they can take home and play again, to refresh themselves about my message."

OTHER TOOLS FOR CASHING IN

These materials offer his audience an extra dose of Vince Poscente.

Radio and Television

Exposure on radio or television is available in most markets. But what kind of exposure is possible? A PR consultant had an answer to this question for a prospective client.

"And get my picture on the evening news," the client demanded, counting off the things he wanted the PR professional to accomplish.

The consultant thought about the easiest way to fill the request, then wisecracked, "If you really want to make television news, kill someone. No, kill several people. If you kill one person, you'll only make the midday news."

The point of this tongue-in-cheek exchange is that all publicity is not equally good publicity. Attempts to utilize the media should begin with research into the availability of the desired media and an appraisal of where the story would best fit. Any story that demands a visual presentation would, of course, work best on television. Examples might be a story on nature photography or an interview with the writer/photographer of picture books.

Some stories are suitable for both radio and television, but research a little deeper. What type of show is best and on what stations?

Make a list of the top radio programs in the area that include guests and then listen to these programs. Just because a program carries a person's name (*The Uncle Billy Show, The Jane Doe Hour*) doesn't mean that the host personally interviews guests. In recent times, talk radio has gone to the "gripe and complain" format in which the

CREDIBILITY POWER

host poses a controversial question and people simply call in during the hour to air their views on that question. It's a popular and inexpensive way to fill airtime.

Some hosts are reluctant to interview authors. Knowing what the host wants will help satisfy your objectives. Most radio market areas have several shows that regularly provide the following:

- A large audience
- An intelligent audience that can follow what you have to say
- A host who is not paid to ridicule guests on the air

The best contact for a certain show depends on the station format and structure. If you are trying to be the subject of a news segment on an all-news station, make contact with the news director. To guest on a talk-radio show, call the show's producer or host. On some small-market shows, the host is also the producer. Some radio stations have public-affairs programs that broadcast at odd hours, usually on the weekend. For most of these shows, contact the program director or the show's host.

> Some stories produce great visuals and are perfect for TV. Study your story and decide which medium it fits.

Television works in much the same way. Most local markets have the network affiliates (ABC, NBC, CBS, PBS, Fox, WB and UPN) plus several local nonaffiliated stations and a variety of cable or community access stations.

Survey the local programming on each of these stations to determine what opportunities are available. Celebrity authors like Colin Powell or Bruce Jenner have television reporters clamoring to speak to them when they participate in events in any particular city. Most credibility marketers aren't so fortunate and have to work hard for the coverage. Sometimes it is effective to tie your writing to a local story that the media is already covering, like the firm mentioned in an earlier chapter does with its newsletter.

Many stories will not warrant prime time coverage. Seek coverage on the early morning, noontime and early evening newscasts, and on hour-long newscasts that need interesting soft news segments. Credibility Power does not spawn much hard news, but what you have to say may relate to other hard news stories. Most of this coverage is on early morning and afternoon "coffee talk" shows. Television and radio stations also have public-affairs programs that air in the early morning or on weekends, and they may be interested in your subject matter.

If you want to become the subject of a TV news segment, contact the assignments editor in the news department. Coffee talk shows usually have at least one booker, talent coordinator or producer to uncover interesting guests. As in radio, the contact for a public affairs show is either the producer or the show host.

Radio and television stations hire experts in various subject areas as regular commentators. The usual TV experts are lawyers, doctors, financial advisers, gardeners and computer consultants. Those who display their expertise on radio command an even wider range of occupations, and more of these jobs are available. In both radio and television, regular commentators are paid for their expertise, but usually they maintain their day jobs and media work remains a sideline.

Most training for radio work is on-the-job. TV commentators sometimes learn through experience, but many belong to national associations that offer training classes for those wanting to become television personalities.

CREDIBILITY POWER

Quite often a doctor who wants to become a regular commentator on a local television station will spend a year or more in classes before beginning a regular stint.

Paid Programming

Appliance repairman Ahron Katz and investment counselor Clyde Goldberg use paid radio programming to raise their profiles in their communities and, as a result, increase their Credibility Power. You can do the same on television, through commercials or infomercials. As the name implies, infomercials are long commercials in which information is imparted. Today, you can sell everything in an infomercial, from the Pocket Fisherman to psychic advice, fitness products to kitchen appliances. Fitness expert Larry North has one of the most successful infomercials, selling a line of exercise equipment. North began by hiring himself out to a production company that contracted to produce an infomercial for a product line.

The most effective infomercials have the highest production values, meaning they are expensive to produce. Of all the credibility marketing ventures, the infomercial is the most expensive to get into place. It's also the most potentially lucrative. Infomercials utilize a well-liked spokesperson, often a celebrity. With the rise of cable and super stations, you can reach your target demographic and speak almost exclusively to those

> **Infomercials are expensive to produce but potentially lucrative. If you plan to produce one, seek out a partner or get ready to spend your life savings.**

OTHER TOOLS FOR CASHING IN

people you have identified as likely to purchase your product.

The cost of a 30-minute infomercial with acceptable production values begins at about $30,000. Add a celebrity spokesperson, an exotic locale and interesting props, and that number can easily skyrocket past $250,000. But production is not your only cost. Airtime in most major television markets across the country can run into the millions. And once the program is presented to the public, you must have telephone call-center workers standing by to take orders and a fulfillment house ready to ship the product.

But with the increasing popularity of shopping by mail order, over the television and the Internet, infomercials can be highly lucrative. The potential for huge profits prompts the invention of many products sold exclusively by infomercial. Selling by this method also is used as a test run to convince retailers such as Wal-Mart and JC Penney to stock certain products in their stores.

CHAPTER 10

IN THIS CHAPTER
- Editors and Ghostwriters
- Literary and Talent Agents
- Collaborative or Subsidy Publishers
- Graphic Designers
- Public Relations Consultants
- Video, Film and Audio Production
- Finding the Right Promotional Hook

Seeking Outside Assistance

Some people can write. Others are persuasive talkers. Still others understand printing or the dynamics of a good seminar. Few people have the skills necessary to be successful in every medium involving the power of credibility. There is plenty of help available to practitioners in a wide variety of disciplines.

> **CREDIBILITY PROFILE**
>
> John Wood had little writing experience when he completed his manuscript. After getting help from a professional editor, Wood's book has been a boon to his law practice.

John Wood was in his early 30s, with a bright future in family and civil trial law. Operating from a downtown high-rise office building in Birmingham, Alabama, he was becoming well known at the courthouse for his likable nature and facility with the law.

He was about to form a partnership with one of his best friends. And he was selected to the *Birmingham Business Journal*'s "Top 40 Under 40" civic and business leaders. Wood decided to trumpet those facts in a firm brochure and other printed promotional materials. And then there was his 150-page manuscript.

Wood had written legal briefs and responses to lawsuits, but never prose for the masses. He knew he needed help getting this manuscript into publishing form.

He hired an editor to help him prepare the finished product, a process that took about three months. The editor began by constructing a detailed table of contents that served as a framework for the text of the book.

"We wanted people to be able to easily locate material on any subject in the book," Wood explains. "By making the table of contents reader-friendly, we were making it easier for the two of us to piece the book together and for the reader to comprehend the final product."

CREDIBILITY POWER

The editor began with the introduction and went through Wood's manuscript one chapter at a time, expanding or contracting as needed, sometimes moving anecdotes or points of law from one chapter to another.

The editor corrected typographical errors or mistakes in grammar and removed redundancies. Since the book was meant for the general public, he retained the legal perspective while emphasizing material that lay people would understand and appreciate.

When the editor finished the first three chapters, he sent them to Wood for his review. This back-and-forth process continued through three full drafts of the manuscript. The editor arranged for the ISBN, registration with the Library of Congress and bar coding. A small regional publisher accepted the book after the manuscript was placed into book pages in a computer page-layout program, and an artist designed and produced the book cover. When it was finished, Wood had the first such book written specifically to conform to the laws of Alabama.

Many authors whose works are picked up by small publishers provide their own promotional services. Wood hired a public relations firm to gain the attention of Alabama readers.

Wood appeared on early-morning television in Birmingham and did a lengthy radio interview, then the daily newspaper ran a long article on the front page of the lifestyle section. He had several local book signings and was asked to speak before parent clubs in the area.

A statewide mailing of the book and an accompanying press release about the book and the author netted several newspaper stories and a couple of book reviews. Wood coordinated a Gulf Coast vacation with a book tour to Mobile, the second largest city in Alabama. This trip produced a TV appearance, a newspaper story and two book signings.

Wood took an active role in the marketing of the book, and that has accelerated both book sales and the progress of his law practice.

Within six months, he depleted his first printing of 3,000 books. Before he began bookstore sales, Wood sent several hundred copies to business referral sources — attorneys in other specialties, family therapists and former clients. In this way, his book enhanced his credibility even with those who already knew him well.

When the publisher ordered more books, a strip was added to the bottom of the book designating it a second printing. A quote was added from the article that ran in the lifestyle section of the Birmingham paper:

> "(This) book has good advice for those divorcing in Alabama." — *Birmingham News*

With more books on hand, a second round of promotional activities began.

Taking maximum advantage of Credibility Power can require specialized talents in addition to your own. Fortunately, many professionals are available in a variety of disciplines to make your CP project a success. Following is a rundown of those talents and services along with an estimate of costs. Costs can vary widely by market size, the availability of services and complexity of the project.

Editors and Ghostwriters

We Americans can be so naïve. Many of us assume that when we see a person's name on a book cover, that person actually wrote the book. But in the case of many nonwriters — CEOs, professional wrestlers, almost anyone famous — a ghostwriter usually handles the difficult work at the word processor. At the very least, the services of an editor are utilized.

Many people who use credibility marketing hire editors to polish their work before self-publishing a book or submitting it to a publisher. For purposes of clarity, we will refer to those who commission the book or do initial writing as author/clients and those who either edit a manuscript or construct one for hire as editors or ghostwriters.

In some cases, editing means simply correcting punctuation, grammar and the occasional misspelled word. An editor's work can vary by the quality (and quantity) of manuscript pages, the temperament of both writer and editor and the expectations both parties have for the finished product.

These situations can be extremely sensitive. The following is an account by an editor of one such writing-editing arrangement. We include this as a warning of difficulties that may arise and to help you avoid overseeing an "editing job from hell."

> "The author gave me a fairly short manuscript. I took a quick look at it and figured it needed a couple of passes of the editing wand and I'd be done with it. The client said he wanted this book mainly to give to his prospective clients. I figured it would look like a book but wouldn't really be anything you might see in Barnes & Noble. That's how I priced the job, with little or no rewriting of the original text.
>
> "But once we got into the process, and the author was getting excited about it, he changed his expectations. He casually mentioned that it should be a book you might buy in a bookstore. That is a different product entirely. The level of

SEEKING OUTSIDE ASSISTANCE

quality jumps immensely when you go from a give-away to something people will pay for at the bookstore.

"With that sudden change, I became more critical of small mistakes and inconsistent writing. I began to whittle the manuscript down to the essentials. You could tell what the author thought was important. He would state an idea once, then state it again in another way, and then repeat it once more. Crucial ideas were repeated at least six times. In several places, I wound up leaving the first sentence on the page and marking out the rest.

"When this first edit was complete, the manuscript was pared down to about 30 pages. I had converted a simple editing job into a massive research and writing assignment. This had the makings of a disaster, so I went back to the author and confronted my dilemma.

"He agreed to pay me a small amount of additional money and to do some of the revision himself. He took his original manuscript and my edited version and brought me back a third version of about 100 pages. He also added some appendix material and several pages of quotes and suggested some additions that required little additional research.

"Soon we had a manuscript that laid out into 232 book pages and about 40,000 words. We had something that was the length of a book. As far as quality goes, I will leave that assessment to the readers."

Before the work begins, the editor and his or her client/author should discuss the division of labor. The most dangerous author is one with no writing background but who takes the author's role too seriously. An editor can do a good job for you only if you contain your pride. Let the editor know any pet peeves you have about uses of the language.

You have to decide why you are using an editor. Do you want ego strokes or a very good manuscript? The very best editors will make the writing sound like you, only better. One editor told us about a client who insisted on starting every paragraph with the word "however," which led to intense battles and a lot of name calling between editor and author. Another editor carried a copy of the *Concise English Handbook* to every work session, because the client said what the editor called correct grammar couldn't be, because it "sounded funny." These may seem like petty arguments, but they can strike at a very personal and heartfelt place for both editor and author.

Remember that most editors know the rules — or have reference books that explain them. These rules should keep you from embarrassing yourself. Nothing is more discouraging than having people come up at a book signing and point out errors in your new book. On the other hand, an editor who will not admit mistakes is not earning his or her fee.

Ghostwriters perform a different, and often more demanding, function from that of an editor. An alternative to the use of an editor is to hire a ghostwriter to compose the book from scratch. In most cases, using a ghostwriter costs more than if you create the manuscript yourself, but often it results in a better product.

Ghostwriters often have experience as newspaper reporters or magazine writers or editors. Maybe they've written books in their own names, and maybe not.

Most ghostwriters can thank Tom Peters and Bob Waterman, authors of *In Search of Excellence,* for creating the concept of branded business ideas. This concept created a need for everyone to have a book and, therefore, enhanced the demand for ghostwriters. Before *In*

Search of Excellence, business ideas didn't lead directly to the publication of a book. They were just part of the culture. Peters and Waterman showed businesspeople that ideas are legal tender and can be exploited for cash and credibility. In his later work, Peters introduced the idea of self-branding, which is the theoretical cousin of Credibility Power.

You may need a ghostwriter to do what Peters and Waterman did for themselves. How the information is gathered determines the amount of work that goes into a book. If you have most of the information in your head, the ghostwriter may simply interview you. Library or Internet research often supplements these interviews. Some of the most time-consuming, expensive research involves tracking down and interviewing other experts.

> **A ghostwriter with good publishing contacts may be more important than one who writes well.**

Once the major research is done, ghostwriters begin most book projects by constructing an outline or table of contents. When that stage is approved, the ghostwriter will dive right into chapters.

While the first chapters are being written, a decision must be made about how the finished book will be published. There are three ways to publish:

- Conventional publishing
- Collaborative or subsidized publishing
- Self-publishing

If a conventional publisher decides to consider purchasing the book, the ghostwriter may be asked to prepare a query letter and a book proposal for an agent or to give directly to a publisher. If you commission a publisher to produce the book at *your* expense, the ghostwriter will simply move headlong through the chapters and get the job done.

A ghostwriter with good publishing contacts has an advantage over others. This factor may be as important as writing ability. A ghostwriter who has a successful relationship with a literary agent or a book editor may be able to get the book published. In that instance, the ghostwriter will prepare a single-page query letter that includes the following information:

- The main idea of the book
- A suggested title
- The book's primary audience
- The fact that the query is being sent to several agents and/or editors
- The question "Do you want to see the proposal?"

This query letter should be sent to all contacts in the publishing industry who might contract to publish the book, and any others who might have contacts of their own. Agents and editors who ask for the book proposal should receive it immediately. The actual book proposal is a document of approximately 25 to 45 pages. Agents and editors want different elements in a book proposal, but most proposals include:

- The main idea or premise of the book
- The book's specifications, including manuscript length in words, format (soft cover, hardback) and anticipated date of delivery of the manuscript to the publisher

SEEKING OUTSIDE ASSISTANCE

- The market for the book, including how this book is different from books already in stores
- Information about the author, emphasizing expertise in the subject area and any writing credits
- Structure of the book (especially important with books that include graphic type elements, illustration or photography)
- Table of contents
- Chapter outlines that run from two sentences to a half-page each
- Synopsis of the book
- Sample writing from the book, including either three chapters or two chapters and an introduction
- Samples of other writings by the author (include any press clippings from the author's other uses of the principles of Credibility Power)

These elements should be packaged together with the title page and proposal contents in bound form. Enough copies of the proposal should be printed to satisfy requests, plus several additional copies.

Your expectations about publishing will determine what happens next, and how quickly. If the book is going to be published regardless of whether or not a conventional publisher accepts it, the ghostwriter should be instructed to finish the project. Some client/authors say that while attracting a conventional publisher would be the best avenue, self-publishing or contracting with a subsidy publisher are acceptable alternatives. The ghostwriter should be told going into the project which publishing venues are acceptable to the client/author.

The flow of work between ghostwriter and client/author is much like that described for a book editor. The ghostwriter writes the first few chapters, then polishes them into acceptable form. Those chapters are forwarded to the client, who marks them up. If these edits are easily understandable and minor, the chapters may be shipped back to the writer for changes to be made. If the writer simply doesn't get it or the editing marks are indecipherable, a conversation may be necessary.

Many people fail to read copy carefully on the first pass. This tendency of the client/author to read with a less critical eye can be frustrating to a ghostwriter, who is getting paid to move the project along and finish on deadline. Nothing slows a project more than finishing a section of copy, then having to backtrack and change significant points in work that is already approved. Read the copy and make those changes as early as possible. The book will be completed more quickly and inexpensively that way.

A ghostwriter must be prepared to accept copy changes. Nobody's perfect, and almost no one can become the client (at least on paper) without some revision. The client/author will have to defend the book and the phraseology used in it during promotional events.

Once the ghostwriter establishes his or her writing voice and the tone and tenor of the work, it's mainly a matter of filling in the details contained in the table of contents or outline. Review the work after every few chapters, to make certain the writer remains on target.

Here are a few suggestions that should keep the relationship with a ghostwriter on a smooth course:

- Before interviewing prospective editors or ghostwriters, evaluate the skills needed to do the particular job. If the book is merely a super brochure, an extraordinarily talented (and usually expensive) writer may <u>not</u> be necessary.
- If you decide to sell this book in stores, make sure to evaluate the person's other writing projects. Has this person writ-

SEEKING OUTSIDE ASSISTANCE

ten or edited other books of this length and complexity?
- Check references. Ask how successful this person's projects have been and how well he or she works with clients.
- Once a writer or editor is selected, mutually agree on a timeline for production of the book.
- Make certain writer and client understand each other's writing and work habits.
- Negotiate the fee upfront, after gathering as much information as possible from others in the field.
- Decide how visible a ghostwriter or editor will be in this project. Will his or her name appear anywhere in the book? Editors are sometimes listed on the title page of the book. If a ghostwriter is well known, the book might be co-authored or written "with" that writer.
- Never pay a writer or editor the entire fee before the work is complete.
- Tie incremental payments to work production. Example: 25 percent at the signing of an agreement; 25 percent at completion of research and approval of the table of contents and first three chapters; 25 percent at completion of the first draft of the entire book; and the remaining 25 percent after editing and rewrite, before the manuscript is placed into book pages. Query letters and book proposals may be paid for separately, when they are complete.
- Commit the agreement to paper. This can be in the form of a letter agreement, which simply spells out who will do what, the time and the price, or as an actual contract.
- Give-and-take between editor and client is a natural part of the creative process. Be serious about maintaining the agreed-upon schedule, but this seriousness should not take

CREDIBILITY POWER

precedence over the relationship. This is a project that demands enthusiasm and pride of ownership by both parties until it is finished.

Cost. Deciding the cost of a book is like asking how much a house costs. You must determine the size of the house, the features in it and the skill and experience of the builder. Most of the volumes written by credibility marketing practitioners identified in this book fall within the following range of specifications:

- 40,000 to 60,000 words
- With fairly large type, use of graphics and some appendix matter or indexing, these books run from 192 pages to 256 pages
- Soft cover or paperback
- Most deal with a single idea

Charges for editing a manuscript within this range run from $1,250 for an intensive proofreading operation to $15,000 for complete editing and rewriting services. The higher figure might include some research but no formulation of new chapters and major subject areas.

Anything more extensive becomes a writing operation. The writing of a 40,000-word book with minimal research would begin at about $12,500 for a writer with no previous book credits. The upper end of the word count, with more extensive research, could double that figure to $35,000 for someone who has a proven track record on other ghostwriting assignments.

These numbers apply to writers with no best-selling books to their names. Writers who produce at a much higher level can demand

SEEKING OUTSIDE ASSISTANCE

higher fees, since their work can be expected to bring the author/client greater sales and the accompanying revenue.

One writer of very successful business books reported that he helped a well-known business figure secure a $250,000 advance against royalties from a publisher. After paying an agent's commission and expenses, the writer took the rest of the advance as his writing fee — about $200,000.

This same writer charges $25,000 to produce a book proposal, but those done by the less famous may cost $3,500 to $6,000. Writers with similar experience may ghost articles in national or regional magazines at approximately the same rate as a book proposal. And some of the lesser-known ghostwriters may even produce copy for the company newsletter at a lower rate.

The charges listed here are for a complete cash-out of the writer. Under this type of agreement, the ghostwriter has no publishing rights and will not receive royalties on the book. Some writers also request a co-authorship or other recognition of their work on the book itself.

> **Offering your ghostwriter a percentage of sales revenue could reduce your initial cash outlay.**

Some writers will accept a smaller base amount for their work in exchange for participation in the profit. Suggesting this type of arrangement can be instructional, if for no other reason than you find out if the writer feels the book will sell. This "cash-on-the-come" arrangement may be especially attractive to self-publishers, who often have fewer resources but receive a larger percentage of book revenue than an author does when using a conventional publisher. The agreement might call for the ghostwriter to receive some money when the work is complete and, say, $1 for every book sold. If the royalty on a book from a conventional publisher is only $1 per book and you give that dollar to a ghostwriter, that leaves nothing for the client/author. Self-published books return several dollars per book, so there is money for the ghostwriter and for the client/author.

Literary and Talent Agents

Many prominent literary agents still work in New York City. When John Grisham or Danielle Steele want to sell a book, the speed dial is set for Manhattan. But for those of us without multiple bestsellers, very productive literary agents operate all over the country. A relationship with one of these literary agents can be helpful in many ways. Some agents are a combination of writer, critic, publisher, talent scout and salesperson. In the traditional publishing arrangement, the literary agent sells the author's book (or book idea) to the publisher and negotiates paperback rights, television and movie deals and overseas distribution.

But the literary agent has access to resources that can help authors finish their projects. Many agents employ editors and ghostwriters or offer those services themselves. Some serve as brokers for book printing companies and as distributors' representatives. Others have their own publishing imprints and publish certain kinds of books themselves.

"We conceive of the idea for the book," explains Randy Voorhees of Mountain Lion, a literary agency in Rocky Hill, New Jersey. "Then we hire a writer, an editor and an illustrator — whatever talent it takes to complete the project — and deliver the book to the publisher. This allows us to control the project all the way through."

With this control, Voorhees doesn't have to rely on the work ethic

SEEKING OUTSIDE ASSISTANCE

of writers he may not know at all. One of the worst things that can happen in his business is to get a good idea from an unreliable author. "It's very rare that someone will sell us an idea and deliver the book with so few alterations to their original idea that the book is acceptable to the publisher," Voorhees says.

Because they have been successful packaging ideas, agencies like Mountain Lion have special relationships with some respected publishers. They still get their share of unsolicited queries from writers. Many of the ideas are not commercially viable, but Voorhees and his associates get excited about the good ones.

Many agencies today seek out less conventional ways of selling books and increasing their revenue. "The agent who sits back and waits for a wonderful book to fall in his lap will starve," says Voorhees. Because agents are out in the marketplace looking for good ideas, using Credibility Power in an effective way can help you get noticed.

Most aggressive agents read newspaper and magazine articles and scour the ranks of public speakers, seminars and workshops for people with unique ideas that could make good books.

Mountain Lion president John Monteleone says publishers are looking for writers with more than one idea on a single subject. They want at least three good ideas that can be converted into books by someone with the persistence, foresight and talent to sustain a Credibility Power venture.

> **The message from agents is simple; Get out into the public with several ideas and those wanting to package a book will find you.**

"We've watched a growing phenomenon permeate the self-help

sector of book publishing," Monteleone says. "We've seen the rise and dominance of gurus, from all professions, as authors."

Talent agencies like Mountain Lion often find those people who've exhibited Credibility Power in ventures other than books. An example might be an author who is an expert in family therapy being retained by a national parenting group to conduct a series of family workshops. Some talent agents operate speakers' bureaus that schedule well-known motivational speakers to address large seminar gatherings or corporate groups.

Cost. Traditional agent commissions are paid as a percentage of the amount negotiated by the agent. For these services, there is no out-of-pocket expense for the CP practitioner. Less traditional services, such as writing, editing or publishing, may be directly billable by the agent to the client/author.

Collaborative or Subsidy Publishers

Milli Brown has been telling personal stories for years. As the owner of Personal Profiles, she is a family biographer. She captures the memories of everyday people and collects them in nicely bound volumes. Many of these histories are given to family members at reunions or holiday parties. Out of her experience telling family stories, Brown wrote *How to Interview A Sleeping Man: 50 Hilarious and Heartwarming Hints To Help You Save Your Family Memories.*

"This book serves a number of purposes," Brown says. "It's a very nice compilation of stories that people can read and enjoy. But it also shows people the quality of book we can do. If you're selling books, what better sales tool than your own book?"

SEEKING OUTSIDE ASSISTANCE

Brown has also developed her own publishing imprint, Brown Books. She works with credibility marketers to bring their ideas and expertise into the marketplace. Brown calls what she does "collaborative publishing," which is a step up from self-publishing and a couple of steps higher than vanity presses on the publishing heirarchy. Brown handles most of these books on a turnkey basis — from concept through distribution and promotion — in the same fashion as a conventional publisher. The only difference is that authors pay upfront for a variety of her services.

Examples of services performed by the collaborative publisher are:

- Work with an author to develop a concept for a book that will best display the author's expertise.
- Contract with a writer or editor to help the author/client.
- Register the book with Books in Print and Library of Congress and obtain bar coding.
- Arrange to have the book designed, produced and printed.
- Arrange for distribution of the book.
- Contract with a public relations or marketing firm to promote the book and the author (some publishers offer this service in-house).
- Obtain additional sources of revenue for the author (these may include author appearances and speaking engagements, selling reprint rights to a conventional publisher, making television and movie deals or selling books overseas).

Cost. Subsidy publishers may be commissioned to handle a book turnkey. Or they may take on only one small part of the process. Most of their services are out-of-pocket expenditures paid for by the author/client.

Graphic Designers

A graphic designer or production artist is essential to many credibility marketing ventures. Agents, subsidy publishers and public relations firms have artists on staff or contract with independent contractors to accomplish a number of tasks.

A graphic designer is necessary to produce the following:

- Book covers and text pages
- Newsletters
- Seminar packet covers
- Audio or videotape labels
- Web sites
- Materials promoting those items above

Advertising agencies and public relations firms employ artists, but many work independently or in design partnerships. To find the designer best suited to the project, ask to see a portfolio of work. Check references of former or current clients to get an idea of the designer's work habits and abilities. Get written estimates before initiating a project and evaluate the designer's work at each phase.

Cost. Most designers charge by the project, based on rates of $75 to $175 per hour. Less experienced people, especially those in small markets, usually charge from $35 to $60 per hour.

SEEKING OUTSIDE ASSISTANCE

Most designers estimate prices by the job. For instance, the design for a book cover may cost $800 to $2,500. This price does not include photography, illustration or copy for the cover.

Public Relations Consultants

Image is everything to the credibility marketer. Creating and enhancing that image is also vitally important. Determine your venture's goals early in the publishing process. If you want worldwide recognition as an authority in your field within a very short time, the media relations effort must be intense. An effort like this demands the assistance of a worldwide PR or marketing firm. Several of the best-known public speakers profiled in this book have followed that route.

Credibility marketers may seek to dominate their field only in a certain region of the country. They may want to stand out in a very narrow specialty. A small regional PR firm or an individual public relations consultant may best serve these people.

> The price range of services designed to ready a book for the marketplace is as follows:
>
> **Ghostwriting**
> (40,000 to 60,000 words)
> $12,500 to $35,000
> **Proofing and editing**
> $1,000 to $3,500
> **Design/production**
> $1,500 to $4,500
> **Printing**
> (10,000 soft cover copies)
> $12,500 to $20,000
> **Promotion**
> $5,000 to $35,000
> **Distribution**
> Percent of revenue

Credibility Power often transforms people into their own best public relations representatives. Insect killer Michael Bohdan has never paid for public relations services, but he has appeared on *The Tonight Show* and many local and regional television shows, and has told his story in newspapers and magazines. He simply studied the media he was interested in and filled the needs of reporters and editors.

Fitness guru Larry North contracts with a PR firm to promote his activities. But he learned to promote himself well before he wrote books, made infomercials and built health clubs. He feels his experience in the field allows him to better supervise the efforts of others.

Learning the basics of public relations can only benefit your efforts, whether you hire PR help or do it yourself.

Cost. Once again, estimating promotional costs depends on the size and scope of the project. The services of PR professionals who work for large firms are more expensive than similar services provided by individual consultants and small firms. Junior PR reps (young, inexperienced, don't know very much) charge from $75 to $125 per hour. Senior PR managers charge their time at $125 to $250 per hour.

Set a spending limit on a PR campaign. Know the hourly charges for everyone involved and insist that the services be detailed in a written agreement and regular activity reports.

Video, Film and Audio Production

High production values are essential to any video or film project tied to your credibility. The perception of a high quality production — in the minds of those people who view your work — can determine whether or not you are considered professional in the message you are trying to convey.

Because of that inevitable transference of quality from the film project to you, you will want to produce the highest-quality production you can afford. A friend with a camcorder cannot adequately capture videotapes for back-of-the-room sale. And the quality of a small, voice-activated tape recorder is not sufficient to record audiocassettes for sale. Commercials or infomercials must match the quality of everything else your target audience might see on television.

To meet the quality challenge, you will have to contract with an independent producer or film production house that will provide a crew and equipment necessary to do the job.

There are many ancillary services that production houses can provide to inexperienced credibility marketers. Those services might include the design and printing of packaging for audio and videotapes for sale; the planning and purchase of radio or television airtime; and use of a call center and fullfillment services to get your products to the consumer.

Cost: Until the scope of the project is known, cost estimates are impossible to predict. But as with any other type of project, the cost rises with the amount of work you assign to your contractor. Some initial research will increase your knowledge and, ultimately, help keep costs down. Much of that research can be done on the Internet, which features sites involved in video and film production and the turnkey production of commercials and infomercials.

Finding the Right Promotional Hook

Timeliness can be as important to enhancing Credibility Power as having a good product and promoting it well. Case in point is Ike Vanden Eykel's book on divorce, which was released in January 1999.

CREDIBILITY POWER

An examination of the campaign waged at that time can show you how an astute credibility marketer, assisted by PR counsel, can aid the promotion and sale of a book. They began by isolating several unique factors working in their favor.

Even though the book is about divorce, it has an essentially positive message — that you can go through the divorce process without destroying yourself or your family. It was ironic that a top divorce attorney was telling people that perhaps they might not want a divorce.

The first quarter of the year is the prime marketing window for books about divorce. People visit an attorney in January, fret about it through February and actually file in March.

To begin the promotional push behind the book, Vanden Eykel's publicist did the following:

- Obtained an up-to-date media list
- Prepared press packets that included a copy of the book, a sample review and a press release
- Sent packets to book editors at the major newspapers in the state
- Scheduled book signings in two area Barnes & Noble stores
- Included information about book signings in press releases to area newspaper, television and radio contacts
- Followed up press packets with telephone calls, setting up interviews and asking for coverage
- Repeated this promotional campaign in other large Texas cities
- Called the county clerk's office in each major Texas city to

make certain the first quarter was the most active time for divorces in that county and included this information in specialized press releases to media in those cities

- As Vanden Eykel made news on television and in the newspapers, used those appearances as an excuse to call producers in other cities and plan coverage
- Added stories and taped coverage of more television appearances to press packet

The promotional push began in Dallas with appearances on the top two morning TV shows and stories in *The Dallas Morning News* and smaller suburban papers. Things were going well. The media was responding to press releases referring to the first quarter of the year as the most active for divorce. Books were flying off the shelves.

Only when they tried to get on the radio did Vanden Eykel and his PR rep find that their timing wasn't perfect. Remember that in early 1999, the U.S. Congress was impeaching President Bill Clinton. When Vanden Eykel's public relations person called one radio station, the news director said the only way the author would be invited on a call-in show was if he had some juicy gossip about Monica Lewinsky and her famous blue dress.

Throughout January, the book campaign fought the president for media time on book tours to Houston and Austin. In Austin, for example, a book signing took place the evening Lewinsky was interviewed on television by Barbara Walters. That was the day before Lewinsky's own book hit the stores. Most of America (including Austin) was at home glued to the television.

Outside of Vanden Eykel's home turf, the publicist repeatedly hit the newspapers and television stations with packet after packet, book after book. He purchased newspapers from every large city in the state to get the names of reporters who wrote about divorce and family issues. He sent press packets in waves, first to the editors, then to selected columnists and feature writers. He sent 17 packets alone to *The Houston Chronicle* by overnight delivery. This helped him score a feature on the front page of the lifestyle section. He scanned television listings to identify programs that might feature the book, then made his way through talent coordinators until he found one who thought she could build an entire show around the subject.

Even with a national focus on the scandal involving the President, Vanden Eykel got major play on TV and in the daily newspapers, including a one-hour appearance on the top station in Houston.

Only a few Texas newspapers actually published reviews of the book. Most considered it a lifestyle story and ran pieces in the feature section.

The book publicist then began to get calls from media outlets in cities the author didn't visit but where he and his book were becoming well known anyway. A feature writer at the *Fort Worth Star-Telegram* asked to interview the attorney about divorce mediation, one of many subjects covered in the book.

"I know Mr. Vanden Eykel isn't a mediator," the writer said, "but he wrote the book on divorce and that makes him the expert." In other words, the book made him well known in a practice area where he was not previously known.

The timeliness aspect — the fact that the first quarter of the year is tops for divorce — caught the attention of the media. They did not catch on to the essentially positive message of the book until late February or early March. At that point, the campaign began to gain the interest of Christian radio.

Vanden Eykel spent an entire evening on a Christian talk show that broadcasts over the Internet.

SEEKING OUTSIDE ASSISTANCE

The promotional campaign continued until his first printing was sold out, except for office copies he made available to prospective clients. He slowed down the PR effort in order to accommodate the clients who came his way because of the book.

Because the marketing of this particular book is so closely tied to the post-New Year's season, Vanden Eykel anticipates a small promotional campaign each year until he decides to publish a new edition. He looks at his book as an investment that keeps bringing him returns.

"I was certain that writing a book and getting it published would have a positive effect on my business," Vanden Eykel says, "but I really underestimated the impact. The expenses of the book and the promotional campaign were quickly replaced by increased exposure and referrals that made me wonder why I waited so long to do it in the first place."

CHAPTER 11

IN THIS CHAPTER
- Making Fame
- How to Secure Media Coverage
- The Basic Press Release
- Make a Book Signing Your Own Private Party
- Newspaper Reviews are Scarce but Valuable
- On TV, Coffee Talk Sells Books
- Making a Plea on Radio
- The Time for Paid Ads
- Leveraging One Medium into Another
- Second Printings, New Editions and More

Boosting Exposure

Because most of us fail to do something new and wonderful each day, it's vital to our use of Credibility Power that we capitalize on the things we do well.

> ## CREDIBILITY PROFILE
>
> Neurologist Dr. Laligam Sekhar was fortunate to have his abilities trumpeted on national television at the precise time that he moved from academic medicine to his own neurological practice. It is a prime example of a media-savvy professional using one spectacular case to boost exposure to his private practice.

Michelle Petersen owes her life to Indian-born neurosurgeon Dr. Laligam Sekhar. In 1996, Sekhar (pronounced "Shaker") performed an unprecedented operation on the teenager at George Washington University Medical Center in Washington, D.C.

Petersen was paralyzed and near death from a brain aneurysm. During 20 hours of surgery over two days, Sekhar cooled the girl's body temperature to 59 degrees to stop her heart, eliminating the brain's need for blood and allowing him to perform a risky aneurysm bypass. The patient not only survived, but she suffered no permanent side effects other than deafness in her right ear.

The operation was spectacular and high risk. The media relations department at the hospital released the story to *The Washington Post* and soon it was the subject of news segments on television and radio stations throughout the nation.

Like many physicians who undertake difficult, groundbreaking procedures, Sekhar has gained a great deal of fame from this operation and the retelling of the story. In early 2000, he left his comfortable position on the faculty of George Washington University Medical Center to form the more entrepreneurial and less financially certain Mid-Atlantic Brain and Spine Institutes (MABSI).

"I wanted to improve the infrastructure necessary for quality care," Sekhar says. "We would eventually like to build a separate neurosciences hospital with high quality surgery and neurology research."

Sekhar built MABSI as an adjunct to Fairfax Hospital in Annandale, Virginia, a Washington, D.C. suburb. It was based on a model of large neurological practices in other parts of the country. "Many neurosurgeons work solo or in very small groups," he says. "I wanted to establish a model of a large metropolitan group that will have some level of independence and yet be allied so we can jointly conduct business of a high quality."

He tried to bring this practice under the university umbrella, but he says the poor financial situation and different priorities of the Medical Center made striking out on his own the best alternative.

It was sheer coincidence that about the time he left George Washington, the Petersen case was reenacted on the medical TV show, *Chicago Hope*. The show's producers saw the original stories about the operation and wrote it into an episode. Sekhar advised producers on the technical aspects of the procedure and loaned them film footage of the actual operation for use in the segment.

Sekhar seized on the opportunity to use the *Chicago Hope* episode to promote his new venture. With the help of a public relations firm, the brain surgeon submitted to interviews with news organizations around the world.

"We followed the same formula we would use with any doctor or other professional," says publicist Matt Hagan. "We're very lucky that Dr. Sekhar is so good with the media. That certainly helps when you are trying to promote someone like this. His situation is unusual, but not unheard of." Spotlighting the spectacular case is often the basis of marketing for the professions, and usually it results in tremendous increases in business.

"One of our objectives is to make more money," Sekhar says flatly. "For that reason, we want to appeal to international patients. With the low reimbursements of Medicare and the HMOs, we can help our bottom line by attracting patients from other countries. If they are coming here for surgery, most often they are very well off. They may have some private insurance, but they are accustomed to paying pretty close to full price for medical procedures."

Sekhar has performed more than 3,000 cranial operations in his career. With some of the most difficult procedures, like the Petersen case, the medical bill can run into hundreds of thousands of dollars. Sekhar attracts such cases by attending medical conferences all around the world. Because of his reputation, he is often asked to address these meetings and is singled out for media interviews.

A major source of patients from outside the United States is international insurance companies. Sekhar markets his services to these companies by writing journal articles, sending newsletters and handling media requests. He is now planning to write a book about high-risk neurosurgery.

For top professionals like Sekhar, nearly all marketing involves the power of credibility. Being good at what he does is a baseline consideration. He cannot be perceived as a good surgeon without *being* a good surgeon. And still, it is important to understand that the hype of publicity is different from the intensity of neurosurgery.

"Watching Michelle's surgery on *Chicago Hope*, I was struck by the reality of the situation," Sekhar says. "I can tell you the real operation was much more dramatic than the television show."

CREDIBILITY POWER

Making Fame

For credibility marketers, professionals in public relations and journalism hold the keys to publicity success. Knowing more about these disciplines and how they react with each other can help you boost exposure. The following story deals with the business of fame. The storyteller, who wishes to remain anonymous, has worked as a journalist *and* as a public relations man. His account of the difficult working relationship between journalists and public relations people tells you how to use their capabilities to effectively generate Credibility Power.

> *"The relationship between journalists and public relations people is a quirk of nature. Journalists don't respect PR people, although some of the best stories in the media get there by way of public relations. PR folk respect journalists, but they are wary of them.*
>
> *"Journalists and PR people are different branches of the same tribe. Journalists are told they might not make any money, but they are doing God's work. On the other hand, the PR cousins make plenty of money, but they feel inferior to journalists and make up for this deficiency with brash talk and expensive suits.*
>
> *"Stationed on the journalistic side of things, I've been approached often by public relations people. A third are accomplished professionals. A third make claims they can't substantiate. The remaining third will sell their mothers into slavery to get you to run a client's story.*
>
> *"But I appreciate being an advocate for something, so I crossed over to PR. The reason for the change could be the big-*

BOOSTING EXPOSURE

ger paychecks I receive for my public relations work. Or it could be my belief that clients appreciate first-rate promotion more than readers appreciate good journalism. To many people, there is little difference between The New York Times and The National Inquirer.

"If anything bothers me about working in public relations, it is the perception clients have of you as some goofy, fast-talking B.S. factory with connections that will get them into the papers. Those perceptions are mostly wrong.

"Many journalists feel perfectly justified being rude and insulting to PR people. They feel they can get away with it and PR people will take the abuse and come back for more. Those in the media complain that PR reps constantly harass them with inane and unsuitable ideas. They claim to turn away 100 lousy ideas for every decent one they accept. For PR people or anyone else wanting to influence the media, realize that you are on their turf. It is your responsibility to earn their trust, even under the assault of discourtesy.

"Trust is the name of this game. Media people must trust that the facts are true in the press release you send or the telephone call you make. They may not know you, but they have to trust that you'll do what you say you will to help them accomplish their task.

"Your job of gaining trust is hampered by the questionable methods of many PR reps. Journalists see those methods in action. When I worked as an editor, PR people lied to me about the facts of stories. They completely fabricated people and places. After they convinced me to do a story, they sometimes neglected to follow through with whatever they promised. The worse the story was, the faster they talked. And if that didn't sway me, they attempted to bribe me with vacation trips, sexual favors or cash.

"One magazine piece I did years ago involved me selecting the top six people in a professional specialty. The magazine was such a valuable display of these professionals' talents that the representative of one possible honoree offered $50,000 to have his client included. Multiplied by six, this story could have been worth $300,000. I didn't bite. The ghost of my college journalism ethics professor perched on my shoulder and that nullified the idea.

"Less-than-reputable PR people poison the well for everyone wanting to gain coverage. In my PR career, I've seen clients attempt to push PR people into positions that compromise their trustworthiness. One client told me that if the facts of a story weren't salable, then I should create some new facts. The expansive egos of many corporate CEOs and other top management people have crippled some outstanding public relations efforts.

"In most cases, you gain coverage by presenting a journalist with a good story that's relatively easy to research and write. Trying to fast-talk someone into covering you or your client is simply annoying.

"Clients get the best results from PR people who have a working knowledge of writing and editing, as opposed to PR reps that are account service or sales oriented. Whenever possible, I place information about my clients in venues that allow me to write the material myself. Sometimes these stories are written under my clients' bylines.

"Most newspapers and magazines run stories from experts who have information important to their readers. Some periodicals even run stories written by public relations people, if the *stories are well written. That practice was strictly taboo in past times, and any use of PR as journalism could get an editor fired. But things have changed, and I would say that roughly a quarter of newspaper and magazine feature stories contain an element of PR or are actually written by promotional people.*

"This development represents a natural melding of the talents and responsibilities of the journalist and the PR professional."

How to Secure Media Coverage

Here are the most important things to remember when attempting to get better coverage from the media:

Research the media you want to approach with your story

Make certain the newspaper, magazine, radio or television program that interests you uses the kinds of stories you are proposing. This research involves reading the newspaper or selections from the magazine, listening to the radio program or watching TV. Just get a sense of what fits where, because no matter how good the story is, few editors will change their format or story mix to accommodate it.

Formulate a story that will sell

The story you are presenting should be a compelling one. All journalists want a story that is timely, pegged to the audience and makes them look good. Think about comparable stories and how they are presented. Don't try to sell something that was in the paper yesterday, unless you can find a new slant on the story.

CREDIBILITY POWER

Secure the correct name and title of the contact person

One radio talk-show host has a simple way of rejecting ideas on the first pass. If she receives material with her name misspelled or with the name of the person who had that job before her on the outside, she throws it away.

She needs some way to cull ideas, and this works as well as any. Personal contacts with media people are essential to coverage. And "personal" means knowing correct names.

Call, fax (or e-mail), call

Every media person has his or her favorite way of getting information from PR sources, but this method seems to be preferred by the majority. Call the media outlet to get the contact's name, title and fax number or e-mail address. If the contact person answers, simply tell that person the information will come by fax or e-mail. Call back when he or she has had time to read it.

Send the material early in the day, to avoid it getting lost overnight. Then call back later in the day, or the next day, unless the person said not to call. Faxing or e-mailing the material allows the media person to know what you want when you call.

Don't be too friendly, and don't argue

Just get to the story at hand. The more "buddy-buddy" you try to become with media people — unless you know the person — the more annoying you will be. Overdone familiarity is the mark of the slick salesperson and is a turnoff. If the person isn't interested, don't argue or try to sell the story anyway. Dazzle the person only with the facts of the story.

BOOSTING EXPOSURE

Get to the point <u>now</u>

A journalist may have all day to do other things but only 15 to 30 seconds to listen to your story. Give the most compelling information immediately.

Emphasize coverage, but be wary of overexposure

There's a thin line between what's hot and what's been done. If the media person's competitors have all covered this story, it's been done. If media in another city, or a noncompeting outlet (it was in the papers and this is TV) has done it, it may still be fresh. If the story has been covered anywhere, look for fresh, new angles. Try to be on the leading edge of thought on a subject, but not too far ahead of the curve.

Supplement the media packet with additional clips

If a media person doesn't bite on the story at first, keep sending news clips or other information. If other media people become interested in the story, sooner or later this target may jump on the bandwagon.

Send the information to more than one person at more than one media outlet

Many stories can fit in more than one section of the newspaper or on different programs at the same radio or television station. Float the story to as many writers or editors at the daily newspaper as it takes to get someone interested. This used to be considered a no-no, because editors in different departments didn't always tell each other what they were going to run and the same story might appear in more than one section of the paper. But editors generally coordinate things better now. Just be sure to tell them the material has been sent to other departments.

Don't take rejection personally

Journalists have bad days, and often they will take them out on you. Just take the idea back to the drawing board, reformulate it and send it to another media outlet. There are many places to publicize things these days. Don't give up without trying them all.

Don't give an exclusive unless it's absolutely necessary to gain coverage

A good story will gain publicity in many places, while marginal or bad stories will die away. There is no reason to offer one editor an exclusive, unless he can offer coverage that surpasses what is available in many venues. In fact, gently using one medium against another is a timeworn public relations strategy. If you can legitimately claim that a competing news outlet is interested in the story, good coverage is almost guaranteed. Everyone in journalism wants to be first. Each wants to "scoop" the competition, and you can help that happen.

Follow through after selling the story

After you convince a writer or editor to run the story, do everything you can to schedule interviews or gather information the writer will need. Be as accommodating as possible and maintain a good relationship with the writer throughout the process. People like to work with people they enjoy. Keeping things pleasant will help facilitate coverage the next time you approach this journalist.

BOOSTING EXPOSURE

Come back with another good story

To journalists, you are only as valuable as your last story idea. This what-have-you-done-for-me lately mentality upsets PR people, who fear they will never establish good relations with certain journalists. That's just the nature of the relationship. PR people are there for the giving, and journalists are there for the taking.

The Basic Press Release

The press release is the most basic component of the media kit for your credibility marketing venture. The following are tips for producing an effective press release.

- Consider hiring a top local freelance writer or staff journalist to write a story about your venture into Credibility Power. Good journalists can bring out the real story of a project, highlighting factors that might not seem important to the untrained eye. (See Appendix B for an example of this from an actual publicity campaign.)
- Take some of the facts from this story for use in a press release about your venture.
- Emphasize the most important facts of your story in the first paragraph of the release and the least important facts thereafter in descending order.
- Make your press release one page, if possible, and no longer than two pages.
- Identify your organization plainly, using letterhead or news release forms whenever available.
- Use short sentences and active verbs. Edit yourself tightly.

CREDIBILITY POWER

Be sure information is accurate and not blatantly self-serving.
- Leave wide margins and space at the top for editing.
- Date your press release for "immediate" use or "for use upon receipt."
- If you use more than one page, place "more" at the end of the first page and either "-30-" or ### at the end of the story.
- Send the release as part of a media kit that includes a copy of your book.
- Be sure your press release is in the hands of editors at least one week before any activity or event you are publicizing.

When your press release makes its way into newspapers and magazines, clip out the stories and include them in your media kit.

For more on press releases and what they can do for you, pick up *Hot Copy!* by Mary A. Mitchell. This 34-page e-booklet contains a short course on writing and placing press releases. It also has several good examples of press releases. *Hot Copy!* can be purchased from Booklocker.com and downloaded to your computer.

An example of an actual press release used by Credibility Power practitioner Ike Vanden Eykel is as follows:

FOR RELEASE SATURDAY, JANUARY 9, 1999

March the Top Divorce Month in Dallas County;
Author to Sign Copies of New Book on Breakups

March is the number one month for divorce filings in Dallas County. Those preparing for the process can read a new book on the subject by one of the area's top family lawyers.

Successful Lone Star Divorce: How to Cope With a

Family Breakup in Texas (PSG Books, $16.95), outlines a more civilized approach to divorce, where couples and their children can emerge from the process financially and emotionally intact.

Attorney and author Ike Vanden Eykel will sign books and answer questions about divorce Friday, January 8 from 7 to 9 PM at Barnes & Noble Bookseller, 501 S. Plano Road.

Vanden Eykel says the idea for his book came out of the realization that people go into a divorce with too little information, too much rage and not enough understanding of the battle that's about to take place.

"I've witnessed the financial and emotional toll that a messy divorce can take on a family, and my hope is that by shedding some light on this process, people may be able to avoid some of the pitfalls," he says.

The period following Christmas is the most active time for divorce filings. "People often resolve to mend their marriages after New Year's," says Vanden Eykel, "but by March they've decided to file."

Vanden Eykel, managing partner at the Dallas-based firm of Koons, Fuller, Vanden Eykel & Robertson, has been named one of the top 10 divorce lawyers in America by *Town & Country* magazine and featured as one of Texas' best in the statewide legal publication, *Texas Lawyer*.

For more information, contact
Publisher
XXX-XXX-XXXX

Make A Book Signing Your Own Private Party

A book signing doesn't have to generate massive sales to be a success. Sales rarely happen in large numbers at these events, except when book buyers line up around the corner for one of the many internationally known celebrity authors who are writing books these days.

Treat the book signing as further acknowledgement of your expert status. Bookstore personnel love book signings. Even little-known authors bring new people into the store, and that makes store managers happy. With that in mind, make each book signing a reception. Invite friends, family and business associates, fellow church members, golf buddies and members of mom's sewing circle. If the signing is in another city, invite business colleagues, civic leaders and anyone else you know or would like to meet. Many of the chain bookstores have budgets to promote these events. Often they will send out invitations at their expense.

Some stores will split the cost of a newspaper ad promoting signings. Some print newsletters announcing store events. Depending on the time of the signing, many stores provide refreshments. If the store manager doesn't volunteer to pay for this, ask about it. Ask about providing refreshments if the store won't.

Authors who aren't concerned about making money on a book should consider donating the proceeds of the signing to a local charity. The charity should send out invitations to its mailing list of supporters, thus helping to generate a crowd. This charitable act should help gain coverage in the local media.

Often bookstores will pair you with the author of another new book to maximize the crowd. You may use these signings as a way to network with bookstore patrons who have come in to buy another book and wind up with yours, too.

Newspaper Reviews are Scarce but Valuable

Like book editors at most large daily newspapers, Bob Compton served as the literary clearinghouse for his paper before his retirement.

BOOSTING EXPOSURE

Each day, mailroom clerks dropped hundreds of books in the editor's cubicle. During the week, books of all sizes and shapes covered his desk and allowed no room for work. Compton usually did his writing at a computer out on the news floor.

"In my last few years as book editor, I got about a thousand books a week," Compton recalls. He and his contributing writers reviewed only about 10 books each week, or one out of 100. That may seem like a dauntingly low number. But the book section isn't the only place in the newspaper where books are featured. He referred many more books to other editors.

"Our big increase over the years was in 'how-to' books," Compton says, "since *How to Avoid Probate* (1965) started the trend. After that, about three-fourths of what we got were how-to books." Many newspapers have responded to the need to evaluate such books by instituting a "how-to" book review section in the lifestyle section of the paper.

Most book editors send promising titles to the editors of various departments. Business writers do reviews of books on significant business issues. The home and garden editor receives gardening or home-repair books. A family editor runs short reviews of books on family issues. Writers whose beats include certain groupings — women, pets or antiques, for instance — collect books until they have enough for a group review.

Some books that defy classification or have good ideas and mediocre writing are forwarded to the feature editor. "Those often get more space than fine literature," Compton explains. "If the idea is trendy or unusual, sometimes it will wind up in the lifestyle section. We met regularly just to pass along those ideas."

Compton says books by authors from the paper's readership area usually receive special treatment. He believes the best way to gain newspaper coverage for a book is to study the paper carefully.

"Find a reporter who does stories about your area of interest," he says, "and you will find someone with a personal interest in the subject. It's effective for you to find that reporter, because he or she can sell the editor on it. Many more stories come from reporters than from editors."

On Television, Coffee Talk Sells Books

Amy Childress is happy to find you. As talent coordinator for the regional television show, *Good Morning Texas*, she has to locate at least 1,500 interesting people each year.

The show, which operates like *Good Morning America* and many local *Good Morning* shows all over the country, contains seven individual segments each day, five days a week. If each segment has just one guest, that's 35 people each week or 1,820 each year.

Take away a significant number of guest spots for reruns and repeat guests and you have about 1,500 guests each year. That's 1,500 separate stories that she digs up by going through tons of material.

"It's basic research," Childress says. "I read newspapers and magazines. I'm on the Internet. And I talk to a lot of people."

Those who become guests on the program are divided fairly equally between individuals who come to her and those she uncovers herself. Sometimes an enterprising author or commentator will call her directly. Others have material sent from publishing houses or public relations firms.

"We want the person to be an expert, to really know what he or she is talking about," Childress says. "Most people come on the show because they have something to promote. We want to make sure they aren't too commercial. They can touch on the product, mention it, but they have to have more to say than 'Buy my book.'"

BOOSTING EXPOSURE

Because TV is a visual medium, every story must offer good visuals. It must be informative and viewers must gain something from watching it.

Guests alternate between nationally known names and local celebrities. The program tends to stretch its definition of "local." If a famous expert on vitamin supplements comes from his home in Southern California to give a talk in Dallas, this is a local story. If a Dallas actor opens on Broadway, this is a local story. In this way, most stories have a local angle and are, therefore, fair game for programs like *Good Morning Texas*.

Like many talent coordinators, Childress prefers to receive information for the show by fax or mail. Stories that look promising are presented to a committee consisting of the show's producer, executive producer and director. Childress' enthusiasm for a story carries some weight, but the final decision is in the hands of the committee.

"We do something different from hard news," Childress says. "We send correspondents out into the city, but the program's main strength comes from having very good guests in the studio."

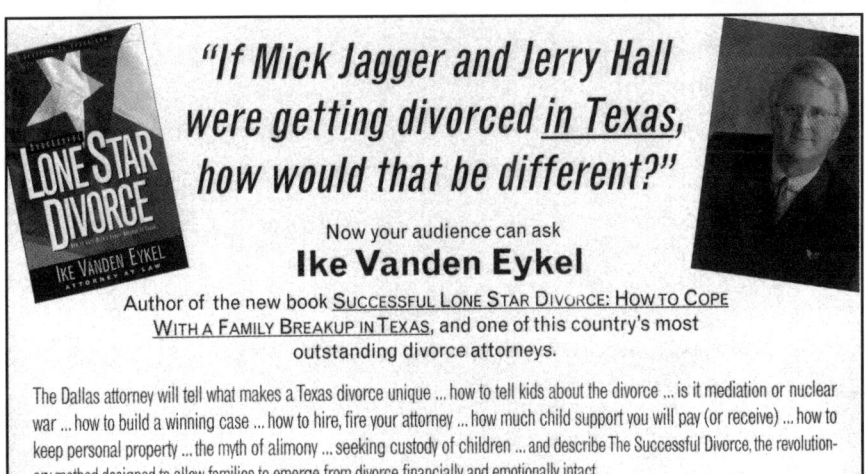

A large postcard, reproduced in canary yellow or bright blue, will get the attention of radio and television programming managers.

CREDIBILITY POWER

Making Your Plea on Radio

In public relations, there is a fine line between being informative and being a nuisance. Either one can get results or cause a radio program director or news director to avoid you entirely. Success in landing a radio interview depends on the personalities of the two people having the conversation and what you are asking them to do.

Radio has been in a maddening state of flux over the past few years. Controversy has overtaken information on many stations. But with the mix of local and network stations as well as cable or Internet-related formats, there are many venues for those who use the power of credibility to promote various ventures.

Getting your message to the program directors of these stations is a major task. Several people sell systems that include primers on successfully using radio publicity along with databases of names, numbers and addresses of those radio contacts. Some of the ideas put forward in these systems are worthwhile. One calls for the promotional team to prepare a "big yellow card" to send to station contacts. Another possible tactic is advertising in *Radio-TV Interview Report*, a magazine that highlights people who are available for interviews. The report extols the virtues of radio promotion, claiming that on radio you can:

- Make sales directly, since many shows will allow you to give a toll-free telephone number or a mailing address for ordering the book or product.
- Get your books or products into more stores by telling consumers to ask for them locally and showing those stores you are serious about promotion.
- Reach thousands of people without leaving home by doing radio interviews over the telephone.

The Time for Paid Ads

While purchasing advertising is not utilizing Credibility Power, buying ads for your CP venture itself can be a wise use of money. Ads for a book, a lecture series, a workshop or the sale of audio and videotapes can be effective means of promotion.

From the standpoint of actual money return on your investment, advertising works best when you are selling a high-priced item, such as a $99 seminar reservation, or expect to sell a number of books for $16.95 each. Even a small ad in a local publication can cost $300 to $500, making repayment on your investment a gamble.

But paid advertising can also sell the services of your core business along with your product, and those potential sales must be taken into consideration. For instance, a financial planner who charges $99 for a seat at his investment workshop might have only four seats left for his next session. Should he risk the $500 ad cost for the possibility of selling $396 in workshop tickets? If his history of placing paid ads indicates that they also generate business straight to his financial planning services, he might be wise to consider placing the ad.

Leveraging One Medium into Another

The boost you receive by leveraging one use of credibility into another is uplifting and often unexpected. The use of their newsletter copy in the mainstream media was a pleasant surprise for David, Goodman & Madole. Dottie Walters' move from giving motivational speeches to scheduling speaking engagements for others was a happy development. Bruce Jenner started on television after winning the Olympic gold medal. Out of his celebrity came work with corporations. And this work has kept his career going even after he no longer produces television shows or movies, or appears on TV himself.

Utilizing Credibility Power is an opportunistic pursuit, and you are there to answer when opportunity knocks.

Second Printings, New Editions and More

If you are fortunate enough to sell all the books you print, or give them away to potential clients, a second printing offers great opportunity.

Second printings don't require any change to the inside text of the book. Concentrate on the cover. Splash "Second Printing" across the cover, pull out a blurb from something nice said about the book and feature it in bright colors. Accompany the second printing with a press release that includes some of the media comments about your work.

If the time comes to revise the book with a complete second edition, highlight the changes that prompted the revision. A new edition can create a demand for a renewed promotional campaign, with more book signings and a new list of potential clients.

BOOSTING EXPOSURE

CREDIBILITY POWER

PART THREE

How to Turn On Credibility Power and Keep it On

CHAPTER 12

IN THIS CHAPTER
- Why Organizations Endorse Outside Providers
- How Organizations Grant Endorsements
- Benefits of Receiving Third Party Endorsements
- Which Endorsements to Seek
- Enhancing Professional Services Marketing
- Book Endorsements
- Enhanced Public Standing

Harnessing the Credibility of A Third Party

Having a respected independent company, group or association bestow its stamp of approval on you is one of the purest forms of marketing. Referrals are the lifeblood of many industries and can be the strongest way to generate Credibility Power.

HARNESSING THE CREDIBILITY OF A THIRD PARTY

> **CREDIBILITY PROFILE**
>
> Insurance agent John Haslett invests his time working with national and local consumer groups. He is paid back with referrals that grow his business.

People are more likely to believe what others say about us than what we say about ourselves. John Haslett has seen this principle in action at his Washington, D.C. insurance agency.

For more than a decade, this insurance agent has cultivated very close relationships with such national consumer groups as the United Senior's Health Cooperative and the National Council on Aging.

"They're based here in D.C. along with smaller regional consumer groups," Haslett explains. "I train their employees on how to compare one insurance contract to the next and what to look for in the policies."

Most of the consumer group volunteers are retirees. Haslett gives advice to members on buying insurance. For the past few years, the emphasis has been on long-term care.

"I develop relationships with the consumer groups and network with the president or CEO of the group," Haslett says. "Since they know me, they ask me to speak at symposiums and seminars for their members. I also work in conjunction with other consumer groups and network with those groups, too."

Many of these groups are hesitant to refer business to outside vendors but are afraid not to help their members. "They don't want to endorse any one product, and they don't want to be involved in the direct-sales process," Haslett says. "But if they don't steer members to a qualified agent, members can end up with an agent who doesn't specialize in long-term care. They can get bad advice, get declined for coverage or buy a product they really don't want."

Haslett often enters the picture after members have bought policies that don't meet their needs. He or another long-term care expert is brought in to clean up the mess. "If consumer-group employees and volunteers feel that I'm credible, they figure I can help their members and be unbiased and not be motivated by greed," he says. "It's in their best interest to get the consumer the best advice possible."

Both Haslett and the organizations benefit from these relationships. He has suggested that many of his long-term care policyholders volunteer with consumer groups. The volunteers hear all of the complaints about misrepresentation, and they are the ones who refer members to Haslett to take care of the problems.

> To gain endorsement by a group, you must show good faith by investing time and effort beforehand.

"I couldn't have a stronger advocate than a client who becomes a volunteer," he notes.

Haslett says insurance agents all over the country could work with local chapters of these national groups. But he believes many of the local agents are afraid to invest the time when they aren't sure their efforts will be rewarded.

"You volunteer your time to contact the organizations, network with them and educate them in the hope that they will refer business back," Haslett says. "Most agents will not take that chance. I invest all of my time in people without any specific obligation. I don't do any direct marketing. I don't have any direct prospecting, no mailers or telemarketing. All of my time is spent contacting people and networking with those who have access to large groups. If I develop a strong relationship, then I feel as though I will be compensated indirectly through referrals. And that has been the way I've built my agency."

Why Organizations Endorse Outside Providers

As John Haslett indicates, endorsements are often given to outsiders because organizations want to provide their members or employees with expert advice, information and services. This is a way to attract and retain members, who as a group may negotiate reduced rates for products and services. The work of the outside vendor may be presented as a benefit of membership in the organization.

The organization may also earn income from the endorsement. Groups often work harder to refer people to a service provider if it has a financial stake in the success of the program.

Financial concessions from the service provider can come in two different forms: discounts to members or a percentage of the profits to the organization.

How Organizations Grant Endorsements

No organization gives a blessing to everyone who asks. Usually, there is a selection process with requirements for recognition.

Some groups have a formal screening process. They may have established criteria that must be achieved. Only vendors meeting the standards are eligible for approval. Other groups may grant an endorsement to those who ask for it. Still other organizations may endorse based on personal relationships rather than formal requirements. It's not unusual for a relative of someone inside an organization to receive an endorsement from the group.

Case History:
Scudder Hits Endorsement Mother Lode

Scudder Kemper Investments knows patience and innovation. Founded in 1919, Scudder was the first investment firm in America to offer a no-load mutual fund. In 1974, after 55 years, its managed funds totaled just $300 million in assets. The company was a well-kept secret in those days.

In 2000, Scudder mutual fund assets totaled approximately $120 billion. Much of that growth is due to aggressive uses of third-party endorsement like the AARP Investment Program.

In 1982, the American Association of Retired Persons (now simply called AARP) began to interview firms to offer investment programs to its 30 million members. It took about two years for the screening process, and the exclusive endorsement from AARP finally was awarded to Scudder.

In 1985, the AARP Investment Program was launched. And Scudder's patience paid off handsomely. By the end of the second year, the program had grown from zero to $2.3 billion in investments from AARP members. The investment program had more than $16 billion in assets under management in the fall of 2000.

Scudder's innovation was critical to winning the coveted endorsement. The new investment program was designed exclusively for

AARP members. Linda Coughlin, managing director at Scudder and chair of the AARP program, explains that service, not sales, is the primary focus. To double-check the service, AARP does monthly reviews and annual member surveys on Scudder's performance. Coughlin reminds us that an endorsement is great, but you must still produce on a continual basis.

AARP's endorsement gives Scudder sole use of the AARP name for investment programs, as well as advertising rights for investments in the AARP member magazine and access to the membership file. With this arsenal of exclusive marketing weapons, Scudder has hit the mother lode of endorsements.

Benefits of Receiving Third-Party Endorsements

Gaining the endorsement of an independent third party offers a number of benefits:

An implied recommendation — Nothing could be stronger than having an independent third party suggest that you can be trusted, will do a good job and will look out for its members' financial, social or physical well being.

Does the group have to come out and say those things about you? Not really. They are implied by their recommendation. If you didn't embody all of those traits, you wouldn't receive the endorsement in the first place. An implied recommendation automatically exists, and with it comes access to the membership or employee group. You own the strongest marketing tool available. It is important to treat the prestige bestowed on you with kid gloves — it's invaluable. Being endorsed by a third party and receiving its implied recommendation is a marketing advantage many spend a lifetime pursuing.

Access to membership files — Another benefit often bestowed on those who receive third-party endorsement may be access to membership files. The list of members may not be available to outsiders at all. If that's the case, you've just struck gold.

This is the perfect vehicle for contacting the organization's members or employees to make them aware of your services. The list will allow you to mail or phone the individuals.

Having the organization promote you—This feature goes beyond having the list of members or employees for your own promotion. Wouldn't it be great to have an article about your specialty published in the group's newsletter or to address a membership meeting? What if the group provided letterhead stationery for a mail-out offer to members, or if it directed member inquiries to your office? Maybe you could even use the group's logo.

Your message has an immensely better chance of being read or heard if it's under the auspices of a third party. Think about the marketing messages that get your attention. How often do you receive obvious solicitation letters that you simply throw away because they have no identifying information that you recognize? Consider how much more attention a letter would get with the name of an organization you have voluntarily joined prominently displayed on the outside. People give more credibility to communications from a group they are affiliated with by choice.

Which Endorsements to Seek

According to the American Society of Association Executives, 44 percent of local associations endorse products and services. A national organization may not be empowered to offer an endorsement, but its local equivalent may be waiting with open arms. Little-known groups are just as important to their own members as large, well-established organizations.

The key is to seek out endorsements wherever they are available. Most individuals don't think to ask. Or if they think about it, they're too hesitant. Some organizations will say no, some will send the proposal to committee and some will welcome you warmly.

Endorsements Enhance Professional Services Marketing

Third-party endorsement is an integral part of professional services marketing. This area includes the promotion of law, medical and mental-health practices as well as accounting and other financial services firms.

The rules of professional services marketing are different from those governing the sale of consumer products and services. Professional services most effectively markets in an indirect and subtle way, relying heavily on third-party endorsement.

Through time, referral networks have been the most effective sales avenues for doctors, lawyers and those who handle money. Those people directly affect our bodies, our psyches, our legal well-being and our pocketbooks. Before we submit to their care, we want to know that others we know and trust believe in their abilities.

When we buy consumer products or services, our standards are not so stringent. We may be responding to a newspaper ad or we may have looked up the business in the Yellow Pages. We just want to know that those products or services are convenient and available. But professional services are so important, and often so expensive, that gaining third-party affirmation is important to our peace of mind.

For that reason, Credibility Power enhances the image of professional services businesses. Take the promotion of law practices, for example. For years, attorneys could only promote their practices through word-of-mouth. In the past decade, some lawyers have begun to advertise their practices. The reaction from consumers and their fellow lawyers isn't always good. Those who advertise their services are mostly thought to be ambulance chasers. Many states have enacted laws regulating the style and amount of advertising attorneys can place in newspapers, magazines or the electronic media.

The conventions of marketing and promotion are not as strict with doctors and money managers. Many medical specialists and those involved in elective procedures, such as cosmetic surgeons and eye doctors, advertise on television, in periodicals and through direct mail. There is less of a stigma attached to this promotion within the medical field. And there is such a national obsession with money management that almost anything goes in the promotion of financial planners, stockbrokers and accountants.

But the power of credibility is especially suited to professional services marketing, with emphasis on third-party affirmation. Whenever attorneys, doctors or financial planners publish books, they will often pepper their text with testimonial copy that implies third-party validation of their opinions.

An excellent marketing opportunity for those in professional services is ProfNet Global, a service of PR Newswire that matches experts in all fields with journalists seeking sources for a wide variety of print and electronic news reports. You can list yourself with ProfNet's Experts Database online at www.profnet.com. Journalists can search the database for the appropriate expert to comment on a specific story. Queries from journalists are e-mailed to those who might qualify as sources of possible news and information on an as-needed basis.

Book Endorsements

There are several ways to invoke the use of third-party endorsements in book publishing:

- Cover quotes enhance the book. The more well known the people are who offer the quotes, the better. But it could be former clients and friends. Make sure to secure real quotes from real people or credibility could be compromised.
- Publication of the book by a conventional or subsidy publisher. This is only slightly more credible than self-publishing. Other publishers, book reviewers, distributors and bookstore personnel can tell the difference but the general public cannot.
- Book signings imply that bookstores consider you credible.
- Media appearances on behalf of the book add credibility.
- Speaking engagements or seminars that result from the book enhance the perception that you are endorsed by the organization sponsoring the engagement.

Enhanced Public Standing

Once you begin to generate Credibility Power, methods that utilize third-party endorsement and enhance public standing may include:

CREDIBILITY POWER

- Mention of the third party in news or feature stories in newspapers and magazines, and on television and radio (essentially positive messages)
- Use of testimonials from clients or others in firm newsletters or brochures
- Leveraging of newsletter stories into the mainstream media as articles under your byline
- Further leveraging of this concept into a regular column or a contribution as an in-house professional at a television or radio station
- Appearance as a guest speaker or seminar member at an event sponsored by an organization outside the third-party group

HARNESSING THE CREDIBILITY OF A THIRD PARTY

CHAPTER 13

IN THIS CHAPTER
- Other Uses of the Internet
- Selling E-Books
- Books on Demand

High-Tech Uses of Credibility Power

New ways of distributing information are constantly coming online. Most of these new technologies are directly applicable to credibility marketing.

HIGH-TECH USES OF CREDIBILITY POWER

> **CREDIBILITY PROFILE**
>
> When two forensic psychologists decided to create a family of publications, they never doubted the ability to produce meaningful content. The question was, how would they distribute their products?

Psychologists Jeff Siegel and Mike Gottlieb are the last people you would expect to lead a technological revolution. By their own admission, they are old school and among the technologically impaired.

Both men have carried on successful practices for the past two decades. Besides counseling individuals and families, Siegel and Gottlieb have served as expert witnesses in a variety of lawsuits, providing research into a wide range of social-science issues. The lawyers they serve use that research to build their court cases and question witnesses for the other side.

Over the years, Siegel and Gottlieb have seen a lot of incorrect, or junk, social science passed off as gospel in the courts.

"An expert witness gets on the stand and makes a claim or draws a conclusion," Siegel says. "Maybe he says that fathers are not as important to children as mothers. Everyone in the courtroom may believe this expert is incorrect, but how do you prove it? If the attorney has the latest research at his fingertips, he can do an effective job of cross-examining the witness. But unless that attorney paid for research on the subject, he won't usually have it available. That's why people can often make claims that have no merit."

CREDIBILITY POWER

To better market their research skills and increase the range of their influence, the two psychologists created *The Psychology in Family Law Digest* and *Family Law Psychology Briefs*.

The two publications were the initial offerings of J.M. Craig Press, the company formed by the two social scientists. Their idea is to take the same research they might do for a single client, circulate it widely and realize a greater profit. Along the way, they want to lend more credibility to social-science testimony.

The two psychologist-entrepreneurs market and distribute the publications as e-mail communications. "We decided to use the Internet because we wanted the fastest way to get the information into the hands of our subscribers," Siegel says.

It's not that either of the principals is a techno-wizard. They were just tired of the traditional ways people in their business have disseminated information. Many journals take six to 18 months from the date of acceptance to publish research.

> **Comparison shopping for technical and creative services can help your venture get underway inexpensively.**

"I knew we would produce a quality product," says Siegel. "We just wanted to make certain the research was not several years old by the time it could be used." E-mail distribution involves less cost than a conventional newsletter, which requires printing and postage. And the text can be changed at a moment's notice.

The two psychologists started by talking with many Internet-savvy people, asking about the technical and creative viability of their idea. "Most people told us we needed to hire an engineer to design a Web site and clear all the other hurdles to make this possible," Siegel says. "So we went out to locate the right computer nerd for us. We interviewed almost a dozen people, and they priced themselves from $500 all the way to $40,000. The spread was incredible, and it shows how audacious people are in that business. We went with the $500 engineer, and it has worked out well."

The traditional nature of social science lent itself to a very conservative design for the Web site. The two sought advice from an intellectual property lawyer and made arrangements to accept credit cards from a secure area on their Web site.

They thought they needed a big national PR firm to help them sell their publications. At a meeting in plush offices in a high-rise building, the reps for a large firm outlined a marketing plan that required first-year expenditures of $75,000.

Instead, the psychologists contracted with an individual PR professional with experience in the mental health field. He produced a brochure, several sales letters, an e-mail ad and a press release for less than $5,000.

"It took us six months from the idea stage to the first issue of *The Psychology in Family Law Digest*," Siegel says. "We developed the publications for less than $10,000, and most of the money went for a tri-fold brochure, engineering time and marketing consulting time."

They had just two paid subscribers when the first issue was posted on the Web site. Siegel and Gottlieb project an operating loss for the first year. They believe a nationwide subscriber list of 10,000 to 15,000 is reasonable over time. If 10,000 attorneys and social scientists subscribe to each of the two publications at $70 per year per publication, J.M. Craig Press could have revenues exceeding $2 million.

After the initial startup, the only real expenses are promotion, Web site production and research time.

Other Uses of the Internet

The Internet is a worthwhile supplement to more traditional means of promoting and selling products and services. Devotees of e-commerce claim that over the next few years, the virtual sales floor will surpass actual places of business in the scope of its sales and promotional ability.

Individual and company Web sites are effective places to sell books and tapes, promote speaking engagements and seminars and announce book signings and media appearances.

Many Credibility Power practitioners post newsletters on their Web sites and some offer streaming video of infomercials or other appearances from those sites.

Some Web sites provide links to other sites owned by CP practitioners. In this way, those who value your expertise can find your products and services at multiple locations. Dr. Phillip McGraw sells his books from his Web site. They are also available on Oprah Winfrey's site, as well as other mental health locations. Amazon.com and BN.com also offer them for sale.

Amazon.com stocks the books and tapes of thousands of publishers. Most in-stock items can be shipped within 24 hours. Authors, publishers and readers submit reviews that are shown on pages that are graphically pleasing and promote their books. This material can be printed and used to promote the book and the author.

Selling E-Books

Readers can now get books off the Internet even more quickly through e-publishing. Many sites now exist that will sell a book and

HIGH-TECH USES OF CREDIBILITY POWER

download it to the buyer's PC, PalmPilot or eBook. Prospective authors can sell their books to these e-publishers under a variety of financial arrangements. Often these arrangements allow them to earn more money than they would by contracting with a conventional hard copy publisher.

Author Stephen King set both the publishing world and the world of high-tech on fire with his publication on the World Wide Web. In early 2000, he offered his 66-page novella, *Riding the Bullet*, for online sale. The same short story could have run in *The New Yorker* or *Playboy* and earned King about $10,000. Instead, the best-selling horror novelist made about $450,000 from people downloading the book directly to their computers.

Less than a year later, the master of horror offered his novel *The Plant* on the Web by a unique arrangement. He committed to publishing two installments of the book. People downloading the installments were requested to pay for them voluntarily. King made it clear that unless people paid for the work, he would not offer later installments of the gruesome tale. For a time, readers responded to this honor system by sending him the requisite amount of money. In the end, this arrangement failed, but it still remains a viable alternative to conventional publishing.

Even without such best-selling authors publishing on the Internet, this distribution chain is becoming more popular.

The whys and wherefores of e-publishing are detailed in *The Secrets of Our Success* by e-writer/publishers M.J. Rose and Angela Adair-Hoy. This e-book can be purchased from Booklocker.com and downloaded.

The book provides all the information currently available on selling e-books on the Internet, along with case studies of many successful e-writers.

CREDIBILITY POWER

Case History:
From Streamside to the Satellite

Credibility marketers are often adventuresome people with a wide range of interests. Sometimes the expertise they display evolves from free-time activities.

For Hugh Gardner, his avocation has become a significant part of his work. Gardner works as a consultant on aviation and environmental issues. What he enjoys most is fly fishing, an activity that fits perfectly with his life in one of the foothill communities west of Denver.

Gardner has fished all over the American West. Years ago, he decided to become more involved in the fishing industry by promoting his expertise.

"Mostly I just wanted to reach a status where I would be invited to fish anywhere I wanted," Gardner says. "But I got pretty deep into this, and fly fishing evolved into part of my business."

Gardner has experience as a writer, so he offered stories on fly fishing to newspapers and magazines. He appeared before fishing groups and even became the editor of a magazine called *Rocky Mountain Streamside*.

These experiences gained him notice among fly fishermen. He was included in a book called *Angler Profiles* alongside such well-known fishermen as former presidents Jimmy Carter and George Bush.

On a trip to the Colorado high country, Gardner came across a small population of rare native trout called the greenback cutthroat. This fish was thought to be extinct for the last 40 years.

At about the same time he made his discovery, Gardner was invited to take part in an environmental grant program administered by a

HIGH-TECH USES OF CREDIBILITY POWER

large national corporation. Most of the money from this program is used to clean up streams and rivers throughout the West. But Gardner had something different in mind. He was determined to bring his environmental concerns and love of fishing together in a film about the native trout.

Together with an established documentary film director, Gardner used the grant money to produce *The Incredible Journey of the Greenback Cutthroats*, a documentary film designed to bring the plight of endangered fish species before the public.

The film was highly acclaimed among documentary filmmakers and environmentalists. At the International Wildlife Film Festival in 1997, Gardner and his film won nine awards. That's more than *National Geographic* or any individual filmmaker. His film was also nominated for a regional Emmy, and that brought his work to the attention of public television stations.

Here's where technology enters the picture. This story of rediscovery and restoration made its way onto public television because of a satellite feed from a nonprofit educational association.

The use of satellite feeds has increased over the years. Today, most broadcast entities send programming to local stations in this manner. Credibility marketers can send interview segments, public affairs programming and infomercials by satellite. Gardner's film was sent along the satellite operated by the National Educational Television Association. Other nonprofits as well as profit-making groups operate their own satellites.

The idea is simple. After giving local stations a one-month notice, the national organization transmits the program during off-peak hours via satellite. If the local station wants it, engineers capture a digitized version of the program and schedule it for their use.

During the six-month period after Gardner's program was transmitted, 24 public television stations ran the program and 250,000 people saw the show. This is a tiny fraction of American viewers, but it's fairly significant for public broadcasting.

"When you do something like this, you hope to affect how people think about things," Gardner says. "But the fishing community is more concerned with recreation than conservation."

Still, the film helped him earn a grant for a native trout education project. He took his film and other materials on native trout into the schools.

"Maybe someday one of the kids who saw my film will remember how we treated these native trout," Gardner says, "and try hard not to let other fish become extinct."

Books on Demand

The term "hot off the press" has a new and technologically more advanced meaning than ever before.

Try this book-buying scenario: A customer walks into a bookstore. He selects the book he wants from a viewing copy or an online catalog. He orders and pays for the book, then takes a few minutes in the coffee bar while his book is being printed and bound. This could be any book, because in the brave new world of publishing, no book

HIGH-TECH USES OF CREDIBILITY POWER

will ever be out of print. In the world just described, books are simply computer files. Bookstores are repositories for those files on CD or by Internet connection to databases at publishing houses. Machines at the bookstores can print and bind them one at a time.

A number of machines now in use produce books on demand. Besides being used in bookstores, on-demand printing is especially attractive to small publishers. This development is a good thing for credibility marketers.

Most books published by those who use the power of credibility are produced either by small conventional publishers or through self-publishing. Even though small publishers usually print only a limited number of books for each title they carry, storage and shipping limitations restrict the number of titles these publishers can effectively handle.

With on-demand printing, publishers have no storage problems. And without storage problems, both publishers and bookstores will be able to handle every book.

At a recent demonstration of on-demand printing, the owner of a small publishing house showed visitors thousands of books on metal shelves in a large room, waiting for someone in a bookstore to place an order. It was a glimpse of publishing's future — a 4-by-5-foot bookcase where he can store thousands of CDs, each with many books on it waiting for on-demand printing.

CHAPTER 14

IN THIS CHAPTER
- Master Your Subject
- Court the Media
- Expand the Franchise
- Stay Fresh and New
- Create Synergy
- Be Realistic
- Live Up to Commitments
- Don't Make Overreaching Claims

Maintaining Success

Credibility Power generates its one-hit wonders, practitioners who make one big splash and are never heard from again. Maintaining CP success over time requires an extra dose of true grit and inspiration.

MAINTAINING SUCCESS

> ### CREDIBILITY PROFILE
>
> No book on the power of credibility would be complete without the story of Mark Victor Hansen and Jack Canfield. Their ability to become successful, maintain their success and extend themselves into all areas of CP practice has made them franchise players in this type of marketing.

The Master Motivator

For more than 25 years, Mark Victor Hansen has built a speaking and writing empire that spans more than 60 separate publications of audio programs, training videos, books, articles, special reports and specialty items. He has addressed 2 million people during 5,000 seminars in 38 countries. He earns millions of dollars each year from motivational speaking and book royalties.

His greatest brainchild, though, has been the wildly successful *Chicken Soup for the Soul* series written with fellow motivational speaker Jack Canfield. They have created the original *Chicken Soup for the Soul* along with additional helpings or portions of *Chicken Soup* specifically for teenagers, seniors, Christians, women, pet lovers and golfers, with more to come.

TIME magazine calls the *Chicken Soup* books "the publishing phenomenon of the decade." At the beginning of 2000, they had sold more than 60 million copies, making this series one of the most successful publishing franchises in the world.

CREDIBILITY POWER

This is a classic case of persistence in the face of rejection. Thirty-three publishers turned down the original *Chicken Soup* manuscript, considering it maudlin, saccharine and "too nicey-nice."

Their agent lost interest in the project and Hansen and Canfield were able to get Florida's Health Communications Inc. interested in publishing the book only because its top seller, therapist John Bradshaw, had just left the small house to contract with a larger publisher. Even so, Health Communications agreed to carry the *Chicken Soup* book only if the authors guaranteed the purchase of 20,000 books at $6 each. Buy-back arrangements like this are not unusual in the book business. In fact, making such a guarantee is a perfectly reasonable fall-back position for Credibility Power practitioners.

Of course, Hansen and Canfield didn't have the $120,000 it would cost them if the books didn't sell, but they believed in the project and knew they could hustle the books on their own.

"Jack and I went to the American Booksellers Association conference with backpacks full of books to sell," Hansen remembers. "Since we know people who do seminars and workshops where they sell books, we asked 100 people to buy 100 books each. We gave away coupons for money off the purchase of books and we sold the 20,000 books before they ever came off the press."

Hansen and Canfield were already publishing pros. They had written a dozen books between them before *Chicken Soup for the Soul* and they believed the book could be a moderate success with the proper promotion. "We did not think from the start that we had a publishing franchise," Hansen says. "We had a book, that was all. And we believed in it."

When the book suddenly captured the imagination of American readers, it climbed to the top of *The New York Times* bestseller list. The American Booksellers Association named it the book of the year. And Publishers Weekly ranked the book second on the magazine's Longest-Running Paperback Bestseller List.

It was only after the second book hit the bestseller list that Hansen and Canfield began to think about sequels that build on sequels that trade off more sequels.

He and Canfield are listed as co-authors of the series. More accurately, they are "co-creators," because they don't actually sit down and write all these books. Hansen and Canfield wrote a handful of the 101 inspiring stories in the first book, published in 1993. But mostly they compiled and edited other peoples' stories, which they work into various themes.

Hansen knows the *Chicken Soup* phenomenon is one that anyone could have created, with inspiration and persistence. The point is, though, that they actually followed through with it. It's all a product of the business plan he and Canfield wrote years ago.

> To Hansen and Canfield, persistence and an effective business plan are more important than writing talent.

"Jack and I have 1,049 points in our business plan and we've done them all," Hansen says. "Now we have a business plan that extends to the year 2020. No one has planned that far out."

CREDIBILITY POWER

To Hansen, staying on course with an effective business plan is more important than talent. That's especially true when the talent lies dormant, as it does with many of those people who say they've always wanted to write, but never do. Hansen is complimented and mildly amused when he is included with some of our nation's literary giants at writing conferences around the country.

"I talk with great writers all the time," he says. "Sometimes I ask them about their business plans and they look at me funny. None of them has a business plan or believes that having one has anything to do with writing books."

What appears to be a spirit of adventure and entrepreneurship is really organization and forward thinking in the extreme. Hansen has harnessed Credibility Power because each of his ventures has built on the credibility he earned during an earlier venture. While Hansen and Canfield excelled as speakers and writers before the *Chicken Soup* books, most of their success has been after the fact.

"After you have a bestseller, people pay attention to what you say," Hansen notes. "You go from nowhere to somewhere in people's minds."

Hansen calls himself *The Master Motivator* because he was able to motivate himself in these ventures as well as to motivate others. He has been seen by millions of people on *Today*, CNN and the Nostalgia Channel, among others. He has been featured in dozens of national magazines and as a guest on more than 500 radio talk shows and is in high demand as a keynote speaker, mostly for *Fortune 500* companies.

Hansen enlarges his Credibility Power by taking each piece of the promotional puzzle and reformulating it into something useful. He is unashamedly promotional and takes every opportunity to sell himself and his products. When asked what advice he would give to others wanting to duplicate his success, Hansen repeats the telephone number to order his tape series, *How to Build Your Speaking & Writing Empire*. This series offers a condensed version of his two-day seminar of the same name. His Web site describes the training session this way:

> Mark Victor Hansen's How to Build Your Speaking & Writing Empire seminar is where a select group of lucky speakers and writers will get to spend two solid days being trained by several of the most brilliant speaking and publishing experts in America! Spend two full days with Mark and his team of specialists in this no-holds-barred, reality-intensive, strategy-oriented mastermind session, and you'll have the knowledge and the tools you need to make your speaking and writing career as successful and profitable as it can possibly be!
>
> By the time you leave this seminar, you'll know more about marketing and promoting, deal-making and negotiating, leveraging and amplifying than most speakers and writers learn in an entire lifetime. Plus, you'll leave with specific strategies to adopt when you get home."

It's been a good ride for a man who went bankrupt three decades ago and vowed it would never happen again. "Our story shows that you must have faith," Hansen says. "The marketplace didn't want us. Publishers and agents didn't want us. Now everyone wants a piece of us. This just shows you how natural adversity is to this process. You often have to walk through fire to get where you want to be."

The Dean of Self-Esteem

Jack Canfield's career is consumed with telling educators, counselors, psychotherapists and corporate managers how to develop self-esteem and achieve peak performance in themselves and others.

He has conducted training seminars for more than 500 schools, companies and professional associations in the United States, Mexico, Europe, Australia and Asia. More than half a million people have attended his seminars, and millions more have seen him on *The Oprah Winfrey Show*, *NBC Nightly News*, *CBS Evening News*, *20/20* and *Good Morning America*.

Canfield has written his own books, including *Heart at Work: 100 Ways to Enhance Self-Concept in the Classroom*. He's produced two best-selling audiocassette programs.

And together with Hansen, he created the *Chicken Soup* series. "*Chicken Soup for the Soul* came about because people kept telling us they thought they had read these stories in a book somewhere," Canfield says. "Really, they just sounded like something in a book. I finally decided that someone was trying to tell me to publish them. It became a divine obsession."

The obsession has made both men millionaires many times over. At the often-reported royalty of $1 per book for each author, Canfield and Hansen have earned more than $60 million each on the *Chicken Soup* series. With such hefty profits, they have hired a staff that gives their Credibility Power venture a structure few practitioners can afford.

Today they receive more than 100 unsolicited stories a day. Staff readers cull through the submissions. Then Canfield, Hansen and a team of co-authors make the final cut down to 101 stories per book, the mystical number in every *Chicken Soup* volume.

Who knows what these two master credibility marketers have planned for the future? But their stories over the past decade have resulted in nothing but constant success.

For credibility marketers, as for anyone, staying on top may be more difficult than getting there in the first place. It demands that you do the following:

Master Your Subject

Some of us succeed through personality, others through force of will. Still other people reach the top rank by hard work. A combination of all three is a winner.

Mastering a subject means staying up-to-date on the latest developments in the field. Don't rest on your laurels. Proceed with daring uses of Credibility Power.

Remember the story of Bruce Jenner. He knew sports and what it takes to be a great athlete. These things came pretty naturally for him. But he knew most of all that he had to master the art of television, and he had only a short time to do it. He approached his task with a goal in mind, and he was successful.

Court the Media

Take a practical approach to your relationship with the media. Give editors and writers a good story and they will respond. They have deadlines and don't want to be bored by a too-long telling of the story. There is no reason to be bullied by the media. Someone will appreciate the story if you are persistent.

Exterminator Michael Bohdan does all of his media promotion himself. The way he approaches his business, he can't afford a PR agent. Fitness guru Larry North outsources most of the public relations work necessary to his enterprise. But he knows what he wants because he took the time to learn what good PR work can accomplish.

Bohdan and North handle media relations in different ways, but they have one thing in common: They both take a hands-on approach, and that is a secret to achieving the electricity of Credibility Power.

Expand the Franchise

Many of the most successful people in this book began with one use of Credibility Power and leveraged their way into others. Expanding the franchise through increased penetration of a subject area is the work of entrepreneurial minds. When Ken Bradford tried to sell his services as a speaking coach, he was hit head-on with the realization that writing a book would give him the credibility he wanted so badly. Many of the motivational speakers we've profiled started with speeches, then wrote a book, then began to offer audio and videotapes and interactive software.

Relationships that do not grow tend to wither. The same could be said for the qualities of Credibility Power.

Stay Fresh and New

"New" is a magic word in the world of marketing. So is "fresh." Keeping your credibility marketing ventures new and fresh is a key to continued success.

There are two ways to keep the freshness. First, you can create entirely new concepts. Carol Miller accomplished this by publishing the book for people wanting to find work in resort areas. Second, you can update a message that otherwise would become stale. Zig Ziglar does it by updating his presentation and practicing what he is going to say before each talk.

Consider how an approach to the use of credibility can be updated. If your cultural references are out of date, saying something fresh and new is a good start. We found this to be true while writing this book. We began to formulate the concept of Credibility Power in the early 1990s. The nation had just come out of a recession. Many companies had just begun to downsize, and there was considerable fear of the future. In the late 1990s, our nation began the longest period of economic expansion in history. The reasons for entering a CP venture changed, and may change even more dramatically over the coming years.

Quick and sure reaction to events we cannot predict or control is needed to effectively use Credibility Power.

Create Synergy

Credibility marketing is often fueled by individual achievement. But that isn't always the case. Jack Canfield and Mark Victor Hansen were successful speakers and writers on their own. But together they created the dynamo of promotion known as the *Chicken Soup* series.

On a smaller scale, psychologists Jeff Siegel and Mike Gottlieb have brought their energies and visions together in a publishing concern. In many cases, one plus one equals more than two.

If combining forces with others creates the synergy that can propel you higher, those partnerships are valuable.

Be Realistic

Not every resourceful homemaker can be Martha Stewart. Few people will hit on a spectacular idea like the *Chicken Soup* series.

There is only one Zig Ziglar, Bruce Jenner and Colin Powell. Many more of us are like Dr. Mark Bernstien. He is happy to do some speaking before potential patients, feel a bump in his income and get the satisfaction of stretching outside the typical bounds of medicine. Pest-control expert Michael Bohdan doesn't even make more money because of credibility marketing, but he can point with pride to his conversation with Johnny Carson and other media appearances. Morris Dees has compiled an enviable record of fighting for justice at the Southern Poverty Law Center. He uses Credibility Power without much thought to making money.

Decide at the outset what constitutes success for your venture. Only then will you be able to tell if you've reached your Credibility Power goals.

Live Up to Commitments

Ike Vanden Eykel tired of book signings about midway through the promotional tour for his divorce book. But he followed through with the signings anyway, and it paid off with increased book sales, more media appearances and increased contacts with powerful, influential people.

Living up to the commitments you make is an important part of any Credibility Power venture. If you commit to helping a reporter with a story, it is important to follow through. If you guarantee to have a tape on the market at a certain date, do what's necessary to get that done. If you agree to show up for a daybreak news segment on television, you cannot sleep late and miss it, because the show must go on.

Being recognized as a trusted authority is best accompanied by the maturity to make the most of that recognition.

MAINTAINING SUCCESS

Don't Make Overreaching Claims

During the 2000 presidential election, Al Gore was criticized for saying he invented the Internet. He became the butt of jokes by stating his involvement in a way that suggested he did invent the system. He was an early proponent of the 'Net, and made numerous suggestions for improvements to it, but he didn't invent it. Gore's claims are a classic case of overreaching and they became a memorable issue in the campaign. With Credibility Power as well as in politics, resisting the temptation to expand on your qualifications is a prudent course.

The more often you are on television, radio or in the newspapers, the more the media will scrutinize what you say. This seems to be a particular problem in the health and fitness category. Feminist author Susan Powter wrote the book *Stop the Insanity* and made millions hawking products on infomercials in the mid-1990s. She was riding a media high until various disagreements caused the media to shine an unflattering light on her accomplishments.

Nutritionist Cliff Sheats, author of the best-selling *Lean Bodies* series, was seen frequently on network television until questions arose about his qualifications. Some health experts expressed the belief that Sheats' books contained incorrect and misleading nutritional information. News accounts claimed that he earned his degrees from an unaccredited diploma mill that shut down its operations in this country.

Sheats sued two newspaper reporters but lost. The controversy led to a loss of media opportunities and, for a time, his disappearance from the media scene.

All you have to sell is yourself. Your qualifications and expertise legitimize you. Make sure that all biographical information is correct.

CREDIBILITY POWER

Be able to substantiate any educational or work-experience claims. Try to curb anything controversial in the way you approach your field.

The more amiable and cooperative you appear to the media, the less they will scrutinize you and the more you will receive coverage in a less controversial way on radio and television and in the newspapers.

MAINTAINING SUCCESS

CHAPTER 15

You've Got the Power — Now Use It!

In the end, having joy, passion and commitment is as important to establishing Credibility Power as being an expert in a certain field. Credibility marketing is a worthwhile form of expression for those people who want to make more money, enhance their status within their profession or make this a better world.

Anyone can use Credibility Power to create a more productive working life. The persistence to follow through with a project is a major asset in this process. A good personality helps. And never discount an abiding sense of adventure.

If the ideas in this book appeal to you, try harnessing the power

YOU'VE GOT THE POWER — NOW USE IT!

of credibility and let us know how well it works for you.

It is our intention to create a series of books and other materials on the use of Credibility Power by individuals in a variety of industries. Personal accounts of your experience using Credibility Power can enlighten potential CP practitioners. And you will receive a copy of the book that contains your Credibility Power story.

To send us your success stories about the power of credibility, fill out the form on the next page and send it to the Partnership for Credibility Power, P.O. Box 795892, Dallas, Texas 75379. You can e-mail us at info@credibilitypower.com or contact us through our Web site, www.credibilitypower.com.

CREDIBILITY POWER

Here's My Credibility Power Story

Name _____

Address _____

_____

_____

Telephone _____

Best time to call _____

Occupation _____

Here's how I use
Credibility Power _____

_____

_____

_____

_____

_____

_____

_____

_____

_____

_____

Tear this page out of the book and send to:

The Partnership for Credibility Power
P.O. Box 795892
Dallas, Texas 75379
info@credibilitypower.com
www.credibilitypower.com

CREDIBILITY POWER

Appendix A

Should You Write or Publish a Book?

Literary agent John Monteleone realizes that writing a book involves more than just the ability to sit down for hours at the word processor. He offers the following test to people who want to write a book that is well received, sells well and returns a profit in its own right.

Look at each of the 10 statements below and rate yourself on a scale of one to five. A score of five means that you agree totally with the statement and one means you don't agree at all. How true are these statements?

1. I have something new or unique to say.
2. I can organize ideas and express them in an easy-to-follow style.
3. I can write more than one book on my area of expertise.
4. I have a track record for helping others with the information I wish to publish.
5. My peers often consult me for advice.
6. I am well known among the general public as well as among my peers.
7. I speak well in front of groups.
8. I have the means to sell copies of my book directly to the targeted reader.
9. I am available to promote the book, including travel.
10. I have access to the media and can reach important reviewers.

Now tally up your scores. According to Monteleone, a score of 35 is needed to consider yourself a prospective author. That's for a conventionally published book you expect to sell in the bookstores. To produce a book that merely serves as a brochure to emphasize your Credibility Power, you should have a score of at least 20.

If you cannot realistically give yourself a score of at least 20, perhaps you should look into the possibility of attempting some other Credibility Power venture.

Not everyone is ideally suited to publish a book, at least not when you first discover Credibility Power. But anyone can initiate some type of CP venture, and that venture can be something other than a book.

Appendix B

To begin the promotional campaign for attorney Ike Vanden Eykel's book, *Successful Lone Star Divorce*, his publicist commissioned this story to be written by a well-known local freelance journalist. The facts from this story were used to write press releases and other media kit information for the entire campaign.

FOR RELEASE SATURDAY, DECEMBER 26, 1998

Divorce, Texas-style has its own rules

"Successful Lone Star Divorce" offers
valuable information for state residents

Fitness clubs packed with the suddenly health conscious and malls filled with grumpy gift exchangers aren't the only busy places come January. It's also the time of year when many spouses decide they have spent their last holiday season with their miserable mates, and divorce attorneys' offices report a dramatic upswing in business.

For those who start the New Year contemplating divorce, following Dallas attorney Ike Vanden Eykel's approach can mean the difference between a new beginning and a dreadful ending. His well-organized, reader-friendly book, *Successful Lone Star Divorce: How to Cope with a Family Breakup in Texas* (PSG Books, $16.95), effectively explains Texas family law in layman's terms, based on a concept that the author calls "The Successful Divorce." It sounds like an oxymoron, but after more than 20 years of handling complicated divorce cases, Vanden Eykel is confident that "success" and "divorce" need not be mutually exclusive.

"The idea of The Successful Divorce came out of the realization that too many people go into a divorce with too little information, too much rage and not enough understanding of the bloody battle that's about to take place," Vanden Eykel says. "I've witnessed the financial and emotional toll that a messy divorce can take on a family, and by shedding some light on this process, people may be able to avoid some of the pitfalls."

Knowledge is power, and nowhere is this more accurate than in divorce, Vanden Eykel notes. He says his goal in publishing Successful Lone Star Divorce is to "inform people, increase their knowledge, and to a certain extent, level the playing field. Sometimes when one of the spouses goes into a divorce with a much lower level of knowledge and input, it makes both the process and the outcome much more difficult. I tell my clients that they are about to go down a very dark alley, and having accurate information is like shining a light in that alley."

Readers are advised how to share the news of your divorce with children, family and friends, hiring and firing a family lawyer, filing the correct documents, mediation and custody issues, asset and debt apportionment, going to court and much more.

Far from promoting divorce, the book may motivate readers to work on saving their marriages. "As people learn more, sometimes it encourages them to try harder because they don't want to go through this," Vanden Eykel says.

Although Successful Lone Star Divorce offers a wealth of practical guidance, it is not intended as a do-it-yourself divorce manual. "When people try to perform certain professional services themselves — whether it's drilling their own teeth or getting a divorce — chances are, they'll do more harm than what they might save in going it alone," Vanden Eykel points out. "My emphasis in the book is to inform people, but also to show them that by hiring a competent family law specialist, they should actually save money. It's a combination of knowledge and getting the right professional to help them make this process less painful."

Texas family law is unique in many respects, requiring specific knowledge that cannot be found in more generalized divorce books. "To my knowledge, this is the first book about divorce that is specific to Texas and aimed at the general public as opposed to lawyers," Vanden Eykel notes.

Besides being a large, highly populated state, Texas has a high divorce rate and an abundance of acquired wealth. It's the only state in the nation that allows custody to be decided by a jury. And jury trials to determine asset value — not a typical procedure in other states — are common in Texas.

Mediation and joint custody are two important features of Texas family law that are outlined in Successful Lone Star Divorce. "Mediation has given people an alternative way to solve their differences. It has been highly successful; the statistics are staggering," Vanden Eykel says. "And joint custody has allowed people to accept that, even after the divorce, children can have two loving parents."

Throughout the book, the author draws on his two decades of experience, using real-life examples to illustrate various points. Vanden Eykel, managing partner of the Dallas-based firm of Koons, Fuller, Vanden Eykel & Robertson, has been named one of the top 10 divorce lawyers in America by *Town & Country* magazine and featured as one of Texas' best in the statewide legal publication, *Texas Lawyer*.

Successful Lone Star Divorce: How to Cope with a Family Breakup in Texas is available in major bookstores throughout Texas.

Appendix C

Leveraging one Credibility Power venture into another is an effective way to utilize CP principles.

The letter on the facing page is a perfect example of how money manager Ken Fisher uses his status as a columnist for *Forbes* magazine to add legitimacy to a direct mail sales solicitation.

Using such effective and well-accepted ways to promote your business is at the heart of Credibility Power.

FISHER INVESTMENTS

13100 Skyline Boulevard
Woodside, CA 94062

Kenneth L. Fisher
Chairman and Chief Investment Officer

Toll free: 1-800-851-8845

Local: 1-650-851-7925

Fax: 1-650-529-1341

E-mail: info@fi.com

Web site: www.fi.com

*************AUTO**3-DIGIT 752

I've earmarked a copy of our most recent *Quarterly Market Report*. I'd like to send it to you free and without obligation.

Aside from not having individual investment results, it's the same report we send to our clients. In it, I give a synopsis of recent market activity and my view of the investment environment for the near term.

With your Report, I'll include additional information and commentary I think you'll find useful. It covers issues critical to you, like the key elements in choosing investment vehicles, the pros and cons of using mutual funds versus private investment management for those investing $500,000 or more in equities, and more.

> Our point of view on issues like these is uniquely credible. I'm an internationally recognized investment expert who's written three best-selling investment books. I've been the Portfolio Strategy columnist for **Forbes** for the last 16 years. And my firm, Fisher Investments, Inc., manages over $5 billion for corporations, foundations and individuals.

Whether or not you're ready now to take advantage of the lower costs and superior service of an investment manager like Fisher, you owe it to yourself and your family to explore this alternative. Return the attached request form and we'll send you our latest *Quarterly Report* and information package. Or call 1-800-851-8845, toll free today.

Sincerely,

Kenneth L. Fisher
Chairman & Chief Investment Officer

P.S. Please reply by the end of the month, if you can. That way, I know the information you get will be fresh and relevant.

INDEX

Credibility Profiles

Bauer, Dr. Robert, 75
Bernstien, Dr. Mark, 151, 158
Birnbach, Martin, 84
Bishop, Bill, 114
Bohdan, Michael, 43, 84, 109
Bradford, Ken, 159
Brown, Milli, 184
Canfield, Jack, 245
David, Clint, 144
Dees, Morris, 46
Dover, Benjamin, 89
Fisher, Ken, 121
Gardner, Hugh, 236
Goldberg, Clyde, 117, 166
Gottlieb, Mike, 231
Hansen, Mark Victor, 241
Haslett, John, 219
Hopkins, Tom, 103
Jenner, Bruce, 66, 78, 108
Kaplan, Benjamin, 143
Katz, Ahron, 109, 166
McGraw, Dr. Phillip, 59, 109, 234
Miller, Carol, 112, 248
North, Larry, 17, 22, 78, 98, 114, 188
Perlis, Dr. Allen, 131
Poscente, Vince, 161
Powell, Colin, 71
Schwarzkopf, Norman, 71
Scudder Kemper Investments, 222
Sekhar, Dr. Laligam, 195
Sewell, Carl, 42
Siegel, Jeff, 231
Simon, Leon, 79
Sperry, Neil, 55
Stewart, Martha, 30, 83, 114
Vanden Eykel, Ike, 39, 49, 189, 206
Walters, Dottie, 51, 78
Wood, John, 169
Ziglar, Zig, 105, 137, 154, 248

Credibility by Profession

Athletics, 66
Automotive, 42
Education, 143
Employment, 84
Entertainment, 128
Financial Services, 121

Health and Fitness, 17
Home Maintenance Services, 43, 109
Horticulture, 55
Insurance, 117, 219
Law, 39, 47, 144, 169
Management Training, 159
Medical, 151, 195
Military, 71
Motivation, 105, 161
Psychology, 60, 231
Public Speaking, 52, 160
Real Estate, 63, 132
Sales, 63, 115

Other References

7-Eleven, 19
AARP, 222
ABC Sports, 67
ABC Television, 24
All-In-One Media Directory, 136
Burrelle's Media Directory, 136
American Society of Association Executives, 224
Baby Boomers, 27
Baker & Taylor, 138
Bowker, R.R., 135
Brill's Content, 32
Buffett, Jimmy, 128, 180
Childress, Amy, 210
Compton, Bob, 208
Coors, 21
Forbes, 121
Gen Xers, 27
Hot Copy, 206
Ingram, 138
International Standard Book Number (ISBN), 134
Kiwanis Club, 153
Library of Congress, 135
Lowe, Peter, 107
Monteleone, John, 183
National Speakers Assn, 54
Peters, Tom, 137, 174
Powter, Susan, 251
ProfNet Global, 226
Radio-TV Interview Report, 212
Ross, Tom and Marilyn, 142
Rotary Club, 153
Sanders, Don and Susan, 130, 183
Secrets of Our Success, The, 235
Sheats, Cliff, 251
Tonight Show, 44
Voorhees, Randy, 182
Waterman, Bob, 137, 174
Winfrey, Oprah, 59
Xerox Corp. Palo Alto Research Center, 75

NOTES:

NOTES:

Yes, I need help utilizing my Credibility Power. Contact me as soon as possible about one or more of the following:

(Check all that apply)

- ❒ Public relations consulting
- ❒ Media strategy
- ❒ Business coaching
- ❒ Agent services
- ❒ Ghostwriting and editing
- ❒ Book and newsletter publishing
- ❒ Speaker training
- ❒ Audiocassette, videotape and software development
- ❒ Media relations
- ❒ Graphic design
- ❒ Workshops, keynote addresses, motivational talks

Other: _____

_____

_____

Name: _____

Address: _____

Telephone: _____

Best time to call: _____

E-Mail: _____

Send this form to:

The Partnership for Credibility Power
P.O. Box 795892
Dallas, Texas 75379
info@credibilitypower.com
www.credibilitypower.com

Do you need help establishing your own Credibility Power?

If you've read the book and still feel unable to utilize the power of credibility, perhaps you need outside help. Fill out the form on the preceding page to contact The Partnership for Credibility Power and obtain help with the following services:

- Public relations consulting
- Media strategy
- Business coaching
- Agent services
- Ghostwriting and editing
- Book and newsletter publishing
- Speaker training
- Audiocassette, videotape and software development
- Media relations
- Graphic design

The Partnership also offers Credibility Power Workshops to teach the fundamentals uses of CP. In addition, the authors regularly give keynote addresses and motivational talks about this topic.

Contact:

The Partnership for Credibility Power
P.O. Box 795892
Dallas, Texas 75379
info@credibilitypower.com
www.credibilitypower.com